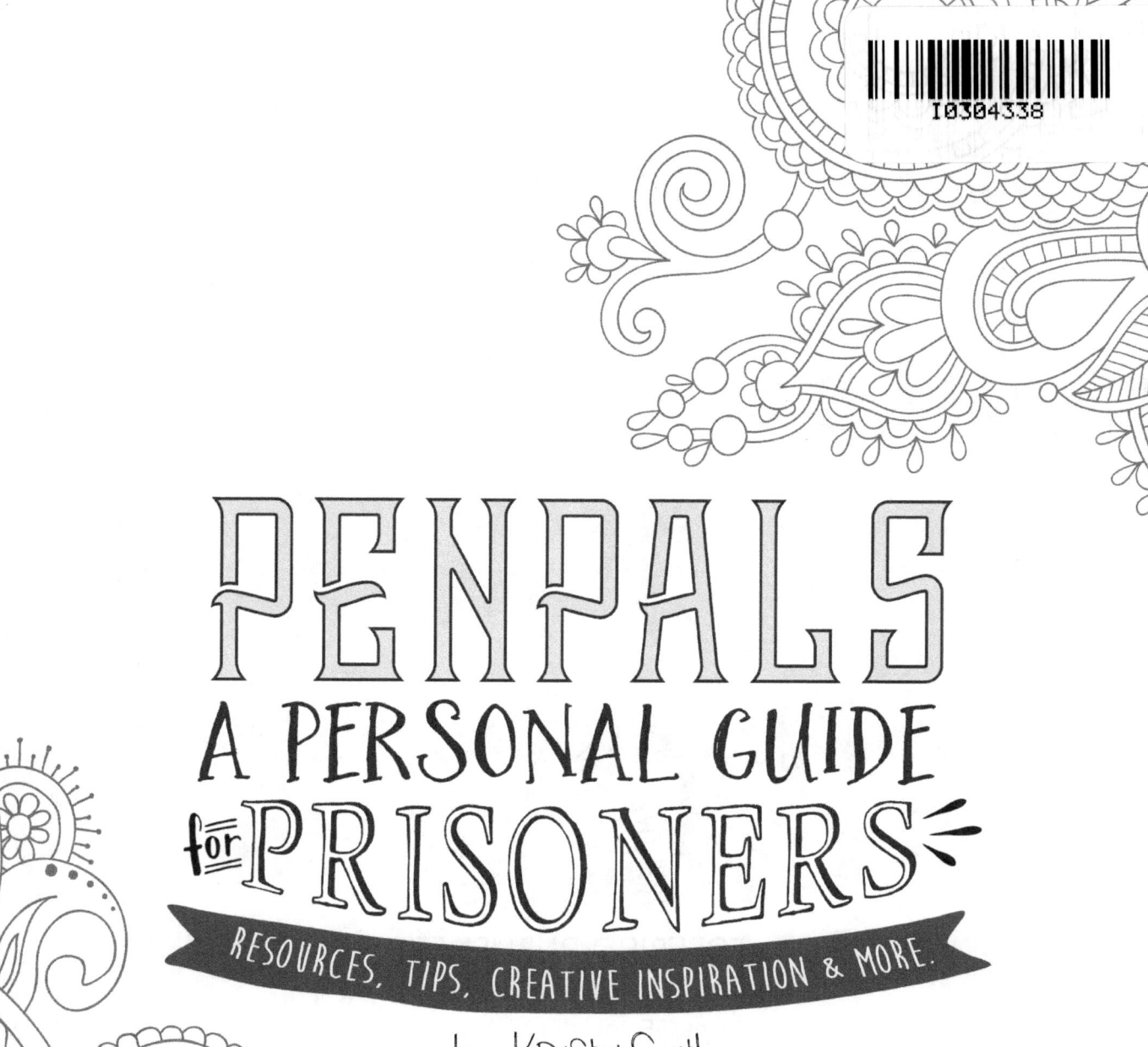

PENPALS
A PERSONAL GUIDE for PRISONERS
RESOURCES, TIPS, CREATIVE INSPIRATION & MORE.

by Krista Smith

FREEBIRD PUBLISHERS
221 Pearl St., Ste. 541, North Dighton, MA 02764
Diane@FreebirdPublishers.com
www.FreebirdPublishers.com

Copyright © 2023 Freebird Publishers | Krista Smith

All rights reserved. No part of this book may be reproduced in any form or by any means without the prior written consent of the Publisher, except in brief quotes used in reviews.

All Freebird Publishers titles, imprints and distributed lines are available at special quantity discounts for bulk purchases for sales promotions, premiums, fund-raising, educational or institutional use.

ISBN 13: 978-09996602-0-1
ISBN 10: 0-9996602-0-9

Printed in the United States of America

PENPALS
A PERSONAL GUIDE for PRISONERS

RESOURCES, TIPS, CREATIVE INSPIRATION & MORE.

by Krista Smith

CONTENTS

PEN PAL PROFILES & WRITING TIPS — 15
- Creating Your Profile
- The Art of the Written Letter
- Writing Your First Letter
- Pen Pal Etiquette
- 100 Things to Tell Your Pen Pal
- 100 Getting to Know You Questions
- How to Keep It Interesting
- How to Find the Right Words
- How to Improve Your Handwriting
- How to be More Descriptive
- How to Start & Close Your Letter
- How to Write a Love Letter

PEN PAL SITES FOR PRISONERS — 45

PEN PAL SITES FOR ANYONE — 55

PEN PAL SPECIALIZED SITES — 59

PEN PAL MAIL ART & IDEAS — 69
- Mail Art & Ideas
- Fonts / Lettering
- Doodles & Embellishments
- Make Your Own Greeting Cards
- Greeting Cards
- The Art of Origami

QUOTES TO SHARE WITH YOUR PEN PAL — 133
- Inspiration
- Success
- Friendship
- Love

PEN PAL STATIONARY — 143

PEN PAL HAPPINESS — 173
MY PEN PAL NOTES & ADDRESSES — 179

FREEBIRD PUBLISHERS COMING SOON...

STOCK TRADING STRATEGIES:

MILLIONAIRE PRISONER'S WAY TO SUCCESS

GRANTED: THE PRO SE GUIDE TO EFFECTIVE PAROLE PACKETS

DNA: THE PRO SE GUIDE TO PROVING INNOCENCE

HABEAS CORPUS MANUAL 2: ANOTHER CHANCE AT FREEDOM

PRO SE GUIDE TO GREIVEANCES: SETTING THE RECORD STRAIGHT

FREEBIRD PUBLISHERS, 221 Pearl St., Ste. 541, North Dighton, MA 02764   www.freebirdpublishers.com

FULL COLOR CATALOG 92-pages filled with books, gifts and services

Now available Freebird Publishers Catalog Vol. 4 We have created four different version of our catalog. Order the correct catalog based on your prison mailroom regulations. Shipped in color unless you request printed in black and white.

CATALOG VERSIONS AVAILABLE (please specify)

A: Complete Catalog Contents B: No Pen Pal Content C: No sexy Photo Content D: No Pen Pal and Sexy Photo Content

Send $5
ADD $5 for Ship with Tracking

ALL OUR BOOKS AVAILABLE AT

FreebirdPublishers.com
AMAZON - BARNES & NOBLE - EBAY
OR BY MAIL: 221 PEARL ST., STE. 541
NORTH DIGHTON, MA 02764
TEXT/PHONE 774-406-8682

FREEBIRD PUBLISHERS, 221 Pearl St., Ste. 541, North Dighton, MA 02764   www.freebirdpublishers.com

WE NEED YOUR REVIEWS ON amazon

Rate Us & Win!

We do monthly drawings for a FREE copy of one of our publications. Just have your loved one rate any Freebird Publishers book on Amazon and then send us a quick e-mail with your name, inmate number, and institution address and you could win a FREE book.

FREEBIRD PUBLISHERS
221 Pearl St., Ste. 541
North Dighton, MA 02764

www.freebirdpublishers.com
Diane@FreebirdPublishers.com

Thanks for your interest in Freebird Publishers!

We value our customers and would love to hear from you! Reviews are an important part in bringing you quality publications. We love hearing from our readers-rather it's good or bad (though we strive for the best)!

If you could take the time to review/rate any publication you've purchased with Freebird Publishers we would appreciate it!

If your loved one uses Amazon, have them post your review on the books you've read. This will help us tremendously, in providing future publications that are even more useful to our readers and growing our business.

Amazon works off of a 5 star rating system. When having your loved one rate us be sure to give them your chosen star number as well as a written review. Though written reviews aren't required, we truly appreciate hearing from you.

☆☆☆☆☆ **Everything a prisoner needs is available in this book.**

A necessary reference book for anyone in prison today. This book has everything an inmate needs to keep in touch with the outside world on their own from inside their prison cell. Inmate Shopper's business directory provides complete contact information on hundreds of resources for inmate services and rates the companies listed too! The book has even more to offer, contains numerous sections that have everything from educational, criminal justice, reentry, LGBT, entertainment, sports schedules and more. The best thing is each issue has all new content and updates to keep the inmate informed on todays changes. We recommend everybody that knows anyone in prison to send them a copy, they will thank you.

* No purchase neccessary. Reviews are not required for drawing entry. Void where prohibited.

Hello

When it comes to pen pals, I've had my fair share and though I'm not an expert I've had many years of experience. No, I'm not a fellow inmate, just an Inmate's loved one. When I was introduced to the prison world I hadn't the first clue. My friend just needed me to be there for him, write him as often as possible, add money to the phone, add money to his books…who am I kidding saying "just"? Yeah, there's a lot that goes along with it, but you know how that goes.

As time went on I found myself needing more money to help him out so he suggested that since I'm a web/graphic designer I put together a website for prisoners who were searching for pen pals. So I did. Penacon.com. Heard of it? Well you should check it out if not. Freebird Publishers has recently taken it over and is rocking it hard core these days. Anyway, in need of finding my first members I decided to join JPay and e-mail some guys to give away free ads. I had to have some members to start with (even if they were the non-paying kind). In doing so I found a couple of really genuine guys who I enjoyed writing.

As time passed I continued to keep up a friendship with these guys (as well as my friend who initially led me down this path in the first place). And in this journey I've learned what it takes to be a good pen pal and what I enjoy having in a pen pal.

There's a lot of guys searching for pen pals…so you've got to stand out. You have to work to make your pen pal happy, keep them interested and coming back for more. If you give them something to look forward to, something to be excited about when receiving your mail then you'll get them hooked…and you'll be receiving more mail than you ever thought possible. This book will give you the resources you need, writing tips, and some creative inspiration as well. If you're looking for a great "How To" book, check out Josh Kruger's Pen Pal Success. It's a very detailed book on how he's been successful in his Pen Pal Journey, you may also find it very helpful.

I hope that you're successful in your pen pal journey!! Good luck and have fun!

Krista Smith

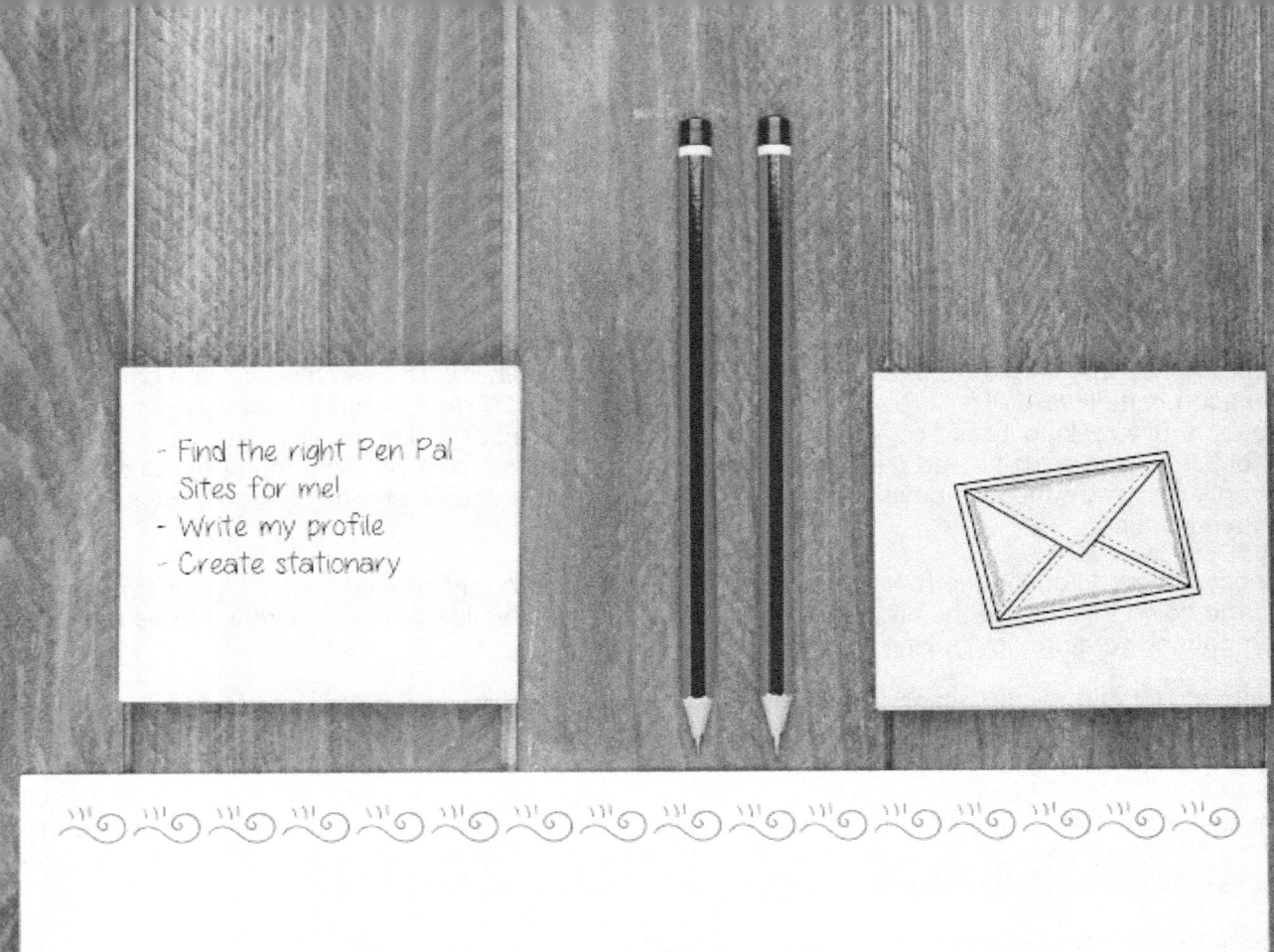

- Find the right Pen Pal Sites for me!
- Write my profile
- Create stationary

PENPAL
Profiles & Writing Tips

CREATING *Your Profile*

Be Positive

Express what you want positively rather than negatively, so that people will be inspired to respond and won't be harboring doubts about your likeability.

Be honest and sincere. Show your wit, sense of humor, or your warm side. Provide information to let your readers get to know a little about who you are and who you are looking to write.

Relationships

Profiles which mention "seeking friendship" instead of "seeking romance" receive 86% more mail (fact on writeaprisoner.com). Keep in mind, most of the best relationships begin with a friendship.

Your conviction

Don't go into full explanation of your crimes or allegations. Your crime does not define you as a person. Your pen pal first needs to know who YOU are, not what you've done. Although a simple statement about learning from your past or the fact that you're regretful of your choices, etc is acceptable, but not neccessary. If you're on a prison pen pal service they already know you have commited or been charged with committing a crime. Save that talk for a more personal letter. Or until they have directly asked this question.

Your Photo

Send a good photograph for your profile. The first thing people see in your profile is your photo. Profiles with photos get many more responses than those that do not have them. The picture should show the best of you. It should show you as you look like today. You can always include other older photos but make sure you have a current one as your main picture. And by all means, smile. You want to look approachable.

About You

Highlight things that make you who you are. What makes you unique? Don't be afraid to mention an interest that may, on the surface, seem insignificant, unpopular or even boring. The fact that you're an avid fan of classic black and white films may not appeal to everyone, but it just may be the interest that makes that special someone take notice.

Mention your aspirations and passions through your profile. For instance, what it is you aspire to do in life, what hobbies bring you the greatest joy, what qualities you value in others. The more important things you reveal about yourself, the more chances someone will read your profile and think "wow, this person is so much like me".

Save your profile for at least a day, then come back and edit. Correct any grammatical and spelling errors. You can add anything you think may make the profile better or remove anything that seems needless. You may need to edit it further to fit the particular companies specifications.

Avoid negative phrasing, it makes you appear close-minded, cold and superficial. Instead of stating: "No old ladies" say something like "I'd love to have a connection with someone around my age." It sounds so much more warm and inviting. And instead of "No non-christians", "My religion plays a huge role in my life" is much more welcoming.

Remember to be you. Let your potential pen pal see what makes you so worthy of being contacted when there are many other fish in the sea of search results. Be unique. Don't just say what you assume others will want to hear.

REASONS To Write Letters

You've already got your hands on this book so it's safe to say you don't need a reason to write a letter, but maybe you need some reasons to convince your pen pal to write? Or maybe you're already pen paling and need further inspiration?

» Writing thoughts and feelings down in a letter makes them known and real.
» Letter-writing takes time, and the process helps us appreciate the people we love.
» A letter is a shared object, and a shared experience that helps our friendships grow deeper.
» Handwriting helps us generate creative thoughts and ideas.
» Letters give us a reason to be creative and expressive.
» Letters can be very diverse–they can include words, pictures, quotes, lists, poems,
» questions and more.
» Letters help us stay connected to people.
» Writing a letter helps us develop our voices.
» Letters give us a reason to express gratitude, which is scientifically linked to happiness.
» Letters let us say things that are sometimes hard to say in person.
» A letter is a more meaningful gift than most material things.
» Letters re-humanize relationships.

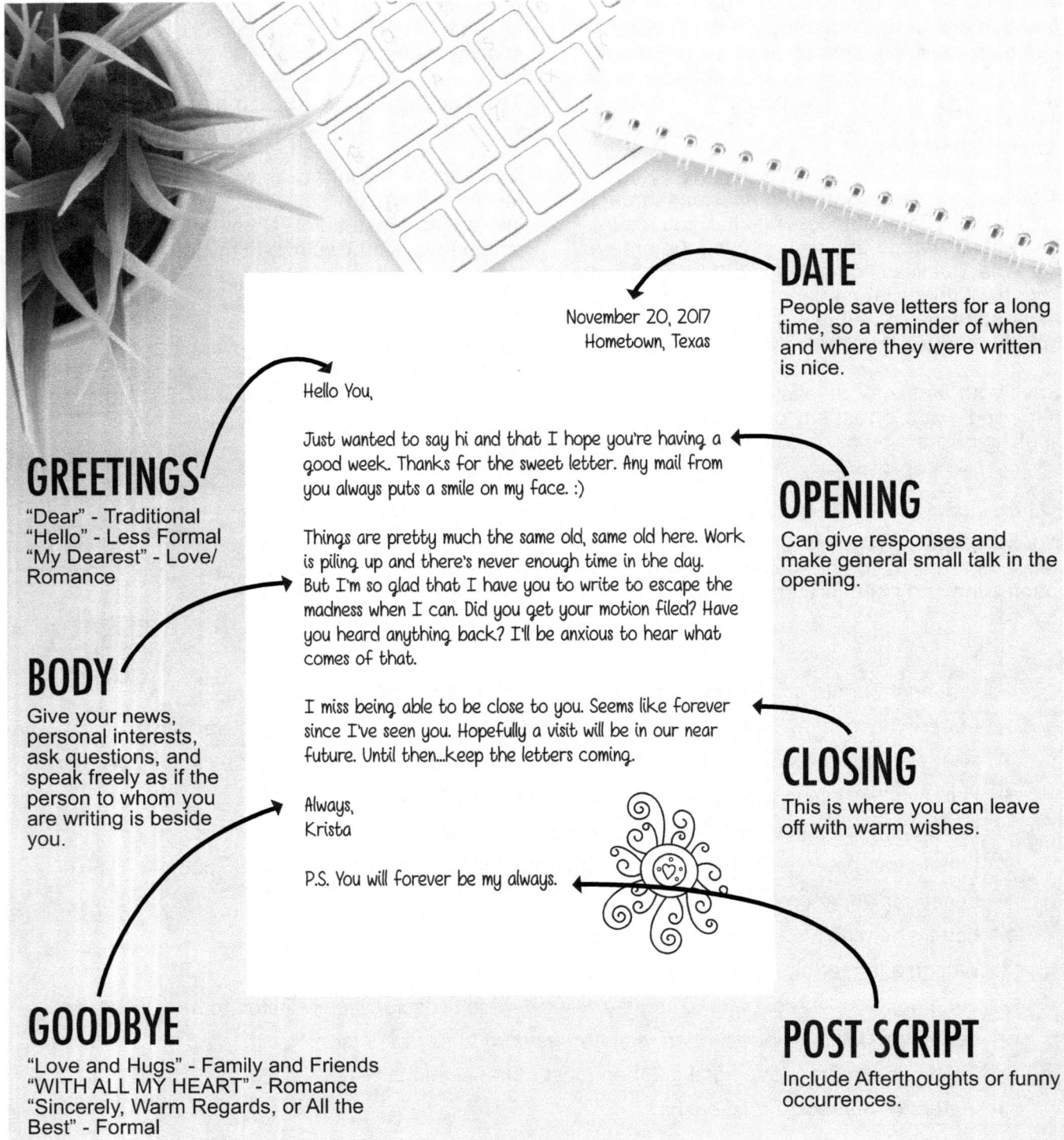

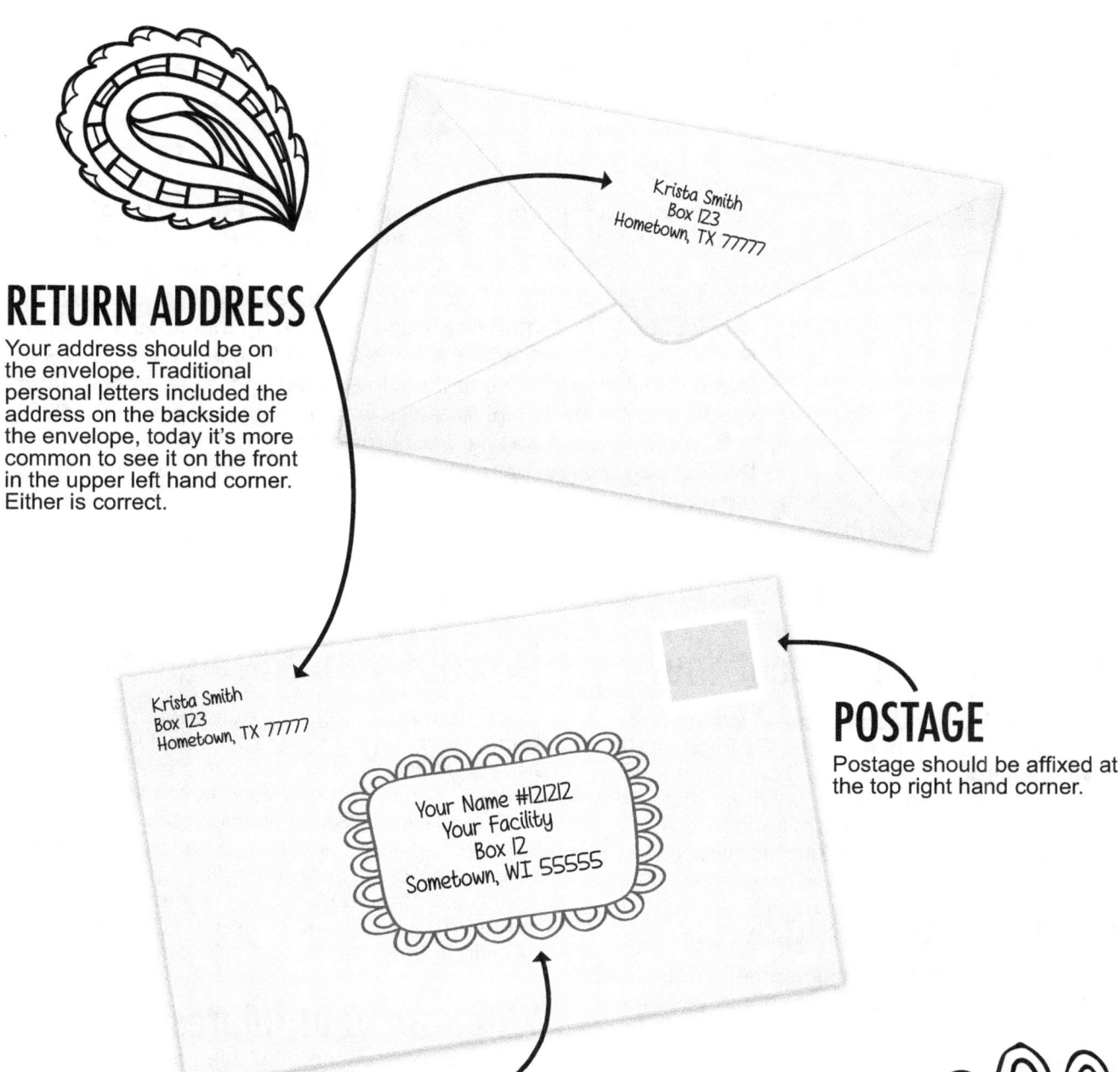

RETURN ADDRESS

Your address should be on the envelope. Traditional personal letters included the address on the backside of the envelope, today it's more common to see it on the front in the upper left hand corner. Either is correct.

POSTAGE

Postage should be affixed at the top right hand corner.

DELIVERY ADDRESS

The delivery address should be in the center of the envelope. Remember to write neatly so there are no issues with delivery!

WRITING *Your First Letter*

When you receive your first letter from a new Pen Pal it's often easy to jump right into responding quickly and anxiously in hopes of sending it off as soon as possible so that you may receive your next letter. Unfortunately, there are many cases where you may write your first letter and never again hear from that special person. Not to fear. We want to share some tips and tricks on how to lock in that pen pal for good. Keep them interested and eager to hear from you time and time again. Afterall it is about first impressions, right? Yes, you hooked them with your profile, but now it really begins... the first personal response they're receving from you to them personally.

Name 10 Things About You.

Weird, small, big, random, funny. Whatever comes to mind at that moment. Example: 1. I have an extrodinary memory, I can remember conversations I had in full detail that I had years ago. 2. I almost always wear flip flops. 3. My mood is easily seen by looking at my eyes.

What are you doing?

Just write down what you see, smell, feel, etc at that time. This will also tell alot about you, in a fun way.

Read and respond!

If after reading their first letter you learn you have something in common, state that. "I like to bike, too, but only on the road. I haven't gotten the opportunity to venture into mountain biking." OR if you don't have something in common you could say "Would you believe I've never rode a bike? I've thought about it, but sadly never had the opportunity." Be sure to answer their questions so they know you're interested in corresponding and show interest in them!

Describe your surroundings.

Many people are very curious about prison living. What is your living situation. Do you have a cellie? Do you sleep on a bunk, top or bottom? Do you have a window? What is the day room like? What is your favorite part of the day? Do you enjoy spending time outside? What is the outside situation like? By opening up the fact that you are okay talking about your surroundings you'll open the door to any questions they may have.

What are your interests?

You can mention some hobbies or activities that are your favorites. If you have a particular goal in corresponding, such as learning another culture or language, say that, too.

Ask Questions?

In the first letter be sure to ask questions, but don't make it too personal right away. General questions about their hobbies or interests are good. Asking questions gives them something to talk about in their reply and is a good way to invite a response.

PEN PAL *Etiquette*

Read The Letter
This might sound obvious, but let the sender know you have actually read it. Answer questions and comment on some of their stories.

Say Thank You
Also seems needless to say, but if you send something to someone you would appreciate a thank you too, wouldn't you? So do not forget to thank them for taking time out of their lives to write.

Write Readable
Grammar might not be your strong suit, but that's okay (you can apologize for it, I do)!

However, make SURE your handwriting is readable do not make it a struggle for the receiver to read it. If neccessary write in all capitals, take your time, do not rush through just to finish and get a letter out.

Make An Effort
You have time on your hands, am I right? Use it. Create something nice for them, something that you would appreicate too. Do not write to pen pals with one thing in mind. Make your mail interesting.

Postage
I know times are tough and money is not always easy to come by, but make sure (especially in the beginning) that you put enough postage on your mail. You don't want your receiver having to pay to receive mail when they're already paying to send mail, do you? It's just little ways of being nice and showing appreciation to your pen pals.

Know Your Pen Pals
If you're writing multiple pen pals use our notes section at the back of the book to keep track of your pen pals. You don't want to confuse them with another pen pal and say something that doesn't apply to them. It can be discouraging to a pen pal to receive a letter with something that is intended to a different person. Use the My Pen Pal Notes & Addresses section at the end of this book to write down important information on your pen pal (ex. birthdates, interests, details about the person, etc.)

Tips
Remember, don't act pushy or place demands on your pen pal with lines like "write back as soon as possible." That just makes you sound needy. And Don't be surprised if it takes a month to get a response. This is normal.

100 Things to Tell your Pen Pal

STUMPED?

Although our introductory letters to our pen pals are usually the most difficult, sometimes you'll find it complicated to find topics to discuss or facts to share with your pen pal. When you're stumped, use these suggestions. Be sure to ask your pen pal to share their feelings on each as well.

1. Places you've traveled.
2. Your family members, and something they each like or dislike.
3. What you'd put in a time capsule.
4. Parts of society that you'd like to change.
5. Things you're really good at.
6. Everything you've eaten in the past 24 hrs.
7. Things that you do every day.
8. Your favorite TV shows, movies, music, books.
9. Unusual facts about yourself.
10. Things that make you happy.
11. Your work or daily duties.
12. What you're currently seeing, smelling, hearing, tasting, feeling.
13. What you collect.
14. Goals for this month or year.
15. Awards you've won.
16. Nicknames you've had and how you've gotten them.
17. Sports you've played and/or hobbies you've had.
18. Your favorite color.
19. Your favorite meal.
20. Your favorite drink.
21. Your favorite season.
22. Your favorite word.
23. Your favorite number.
24. Your favorite holiday.
25. Your favorite quote.

26. Your favorite superhero.
27. The type of letters/mail you like to recieve.
28. The most adventurous thing you've ever done.
29. Whether you believe in God, ghosts, aliens, magic.
30. How tall you are.
31. When is your birthday?
32. What is the last movie you've watched?
33. How would you describe your fashion style?
34. Your life story in six words.
35. What shoes you wear the most.
36. Any fears you have.
37. What were you like in high school?
38. Weird/awkward dates you've been on.
39. Something illegal you've done.
40. Why you like mail.
41. The silliest thing you did in the past week.
42. What you would wish for right now.
43. The best job you ever had.
44. A funny and embarrassing story.
45. Something silly you thought was true as a child.
46. What you'd do at your wedding.
47. A time you met someone famous.
48. Something you wish you had done in the past but didn't.
49. If you spent the day at a beach, what activities would you partake in?
50. What kind of dreams do you have (non-sexual)?
51. The last time you did something new for the first time.
52. The kindest thing a stranger has ever done for you.
53. The kindest thing you have ever done for a stranger.
54. Places you'd like to travel.
55. Your guilty pleasures.
56. How you procrastinate.
57. Your tattoos, peircings, birthmarks, scars, etc.
58. Your nervous habits.
59. Areas of life you're confident enough to give advice in.
60. Your pet peeves.
61. What you'd want to do if you were in New York City for a day.
62. Your ideal party.
63. Something that cheers you up without fail.
64. How you sleep at night (clothes, doors, temperature, sleep positions, etc).
65. How you store your recieved mail.
66. Do you believe in fate, destiny or luck?
67. What you thought you'd be when you grew up.
68. Your heritage.
69. What you're attracted to in a new friend (or romantic partner).
70. Do you sing in the shower?
71. The best piece of mail you've ever received.
72. Do you dance?
73. Have you ever done anything that made your stomach flip?
74. One thing in your day that you can't live without.
75. A food you absolutely hate.
76. What are you most grateful for in your life?
77. Three things you have faith in.
78. If you could read one persons mind, who would it be?
79. Did you thank anyone today?
80. To whom is the last person you said 'I Love You'?
81. On a scale from 1-10 how clean do you keep your home?
82. What did you find inspiring today?
83. Something you are proud of.
84. Something you are ashamed of.
85. Something you regret.
86. Your favorite part or time period in your life.
87. Strangest job you ever had.
88. 5 passions you have.
89. 3 significant memories from your childhood.
90. 5 people who have influenced you.
91. 3 legitimate fears.
92. 5 hobbies.
93. What do you think people misunderstand the most about you?
94. Pet peeves.
95. A drunken story.
96. Last argument you had.
97. Something you are currently worrying about.
98. A song (and the lyrics) that apply to your current feelings.
99. How would you spend $10,000?
100. If you won the lottery...

100 Getting to Know You Questions

It's tough getting to know someone especially when you're not sitting in front of them. Here are some questions you can ask your pen pal to get to know them better. Remember in asking these questions it's also polite to share your answers as well.

1. Who is your hero?
2. If you could live anywhere, where would it be?
3. What is your biggest fear?
4. What is your favorite family vacation?
5. What would you change about yourself if you could?
6. What really makes you angry?
7. What motivates you to work hard?
8. What is your biggest complaint about your current living situation?
9. What is your proudest accomplishment?
10. What is your favorite childhood memory?
11. What is your favorite book?
12. What makes you laugh the most?
13. If you could choose to do anything for a day, what would it be?
14. If you could choose to be anyone else for the day, who would you chose to be and why?
15. What is your favorite sport to watch?
16. Do you have any favorite sports teams?
17. Would you rather ride a bike, ride a horse, or drive a car?
18. What would you sing at Karaoke night?
19. What type of music do you listen to?
20. Which would you rather do: wash dishes, mow the lawn, clean the bathroom or vaccuum the house?
21. If you could only eat one meal for the rest of your life, what would it be?
22. Who is your favorite author?
23. Do you like or dislike surprises?
24. In the evening would you rather hang with friends, play a game, visit a relative, watch a movie, or read?

25. Would you rather vacation in Hawaii or Alsaska? and why?
26. Would you rather win the lottery or work at the perfect job? and why?
27. Who would you want to be stranded with on a deserted island?
28. If money was no object, what would you do all day?
29. If you could go back in time, what year would you travel to? and why?
30. How would your friends describe you?
31. What are your hobbies?
32. What is the best gift you've ever received?
33. What is the best gift you've ever given?
34. Aside from the necessities, what one thing could you not go a day without?
35. Where do you see yourself in five years?
36. What would you do if you won the lottery?
37. What form of public transportation do you prefer? (air, boat, train, bus, car, edtc.)
38. What is your favorite animal?
39. If you could go back in time and change one thing, what would it be?
40. If you could share a meal with any four individuals, living or dead, who would they be and why?
41. How many pillows do you sleep with?
42. What is the longest you've gone without sleep and why?
43. Would you rather trade intelligence for looks or looks for intelligence?
44. What is your favorite holiday?
45. What is the most daring thing you've ever done?
46. What was the last thing you recorded on TV?
47. What was the last book you read?
48. What is your favorite type of foreign food?
49. Are you a clean or messy person?
50. How long does it take you to get ready in the morning?
51. If you had to choose someone to play you in a movie of your life, who would it be?
52. What is your favorite fast food chain?
53. Do you love or hate rollercoasters?
54. What is your favorite family tradition?
55. What is your favorite movie?
56. How old where you when you learned Santa wasn't real? How did you find out?
57. Is your glass half full or half empty?
58. What is the craziest thing you've done in the name of love?
59. What three items would you take with you on a deserted island?
60. What was your favorite subject in school?
61. What is the most unusual thing you've ever eaten?
62. Do you collect anything?
63. Is there anything you wished would come back into fashion?
64. Which of the five senses would you say is your strongest?
65. Have you ever been given a surprise party?
66. What do you do to keep fit?
67. If you were the ruler of your own country what would be the first law you would introduce?
68. Who was your favorite teacher in school and why?
69. What three things do you think of most each day?
70. If you had a warning label, what would yours say?
71. What song would you say best sums you up?
72. What celebrity would you like to meet at Starbucks for a cup of coffee?
73. What do you order at starbucks?
74. Who was your first crush?
75. What is the most interesting thing you can see out of your window?
76. What was your first job?
77. How many and what languages can you speak?
78. Who is the most intelligent person you know?
79. If you had to describe yourself as an animal, which one would it be?
80. What is one thing you will never do again?
81. Who knows you the best?
82. What do you define as family?
83. If you could live forever, how would you spend eternity?

84. How would you spend a billion dollars?
85. In what ways do you hold yourself back?
86. How do you want to be remembered?
87. In what ways are you a leader? In what ways are you a follower?
88. If you could change one law what would it be and why?
89. What is your greatest failure and how did you overcome it?
90. What is your greatest achievement and how has it shaped you?
91. If you could master one skill you don't have right now, what would it be?
92. Which are you more likely to fight for, money or love? and why?
93. What would be your "perfect" date?
94. If you could have one super power what would it be and how would you use it?
95. Would you rather be a jack of many trades or the master of one?
96. What is "home" to you?
97. What motivates you to succeed?
98. If you could choose your last words, what would they be?
99. How do you define love?
100. What words of wisdom would you pass on to your childhood self?

FACTS 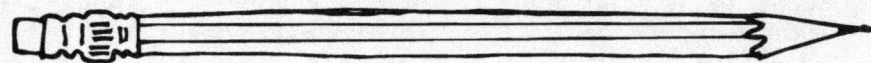 About Letter Writing

- The motion of your hand as you write calms the nervous system and forges important creative connections, engages your motor skills, and keeps your mind sharp.

- Once the mind and motor co-ordination is established properly and the motor becomes automated the student's mind is liberated to implement new ideas more creatively and effectively.

- Slow Hand writers have problems of poor mind motor co-ordination, spellings, word formation, letter creation and discrimination between upper and lower case.

- Areas of your brain light up when you write words by hand versus just studying the words closely.

- Knowing someone's handwriting can be a marker of a frienship's longevity.

- The average no. 2 pencil can draw a line 35 miles long, the average ball point pen will only get you about 5 miles.

- Handwriting identifies to the conscious and subconscious traits of an individual's personality. If anyone struggles with handwriting, they suffer from the ability of self expression.

- Handwriting is a brain's writing. One can judge an individual's state of mind and personality from his style of writing, pressure, slants, space and margin formation etc. differs every time and narrates a different story about the writer.

Freebird Publishers
Post-Conviction Relief Series

Post-Conviction Relief Books

⇒ Secrets Exposed
⇒ The Appeal
⇒ Advancing Your Claim
⇒ Winning Claims
⇒ C.O.A. in the Supreme Court
⇒ Post-Conviction Relief Second Last Chance

JUST ARRIVED

Post-Conviction Relief: The Advocate

Each Only $28.99 Includes S/H with tracking

Post-Conviction Relief is a subject most often pursued only by prisoners, the people who are most deprived of the necessary information. What is offered in most law libraries, is in inadequate, because what is needed is watered down by piles of useless and confusing information. That's why the Post-Conviction Relief series was written. It is a no-nonsense guide, to legal research, that is written in a language that anyone can understand. Most importantly, each book has been written to serve a specific purpose, as instructions for a specific step in the Post-Conviction process. With this collection of books, the average person can quickly become a more powerful advocate than they have ever been before, even if only on their own case. Within this set of books, the reader will find that there is something for all prisoners, whether it's their first day in prison or their first day of supervised release.

★ The best instruction one can receive is the words of experience. The Post-Conviction Relief series is written by a real advocate who has actually been there and prevailed in many cases.
★ In most cases prisoners have only one year to make their claims, the Post-Conviction Relief series is the no-nonsense path to understanding the process.
★ The Post-Conviction Relief series provides its readers with the court rules that pertain to Post Conviction Relief. A great resource for prisoners who are often locked down.
★ Post-Conviction Relief: you want to succeed, follow my lead.
★ All books are not created equal. Get only what you need with the Post-Conviction Relief series.

All Books Softcover, 8x10", B&W, 190+ pages EACH $28.99 includes s/h with tracking

Written in simple terms for everyone to understand, it's not just for lawyers anymore.

NO ORDER FORM NEEDED CLEARLY WRITE ON PAPER & SEND PAYMENT TO:
Freebird Publishers 221 Pearl St., Ste. 541, North Dighton, MA 02764
Diane@FreebirdPublishers.com   www.FreebirdPublishers.com
Toll Free: 888-712-1987   Text/Phone: 774-406-8682

We Accept All Forms of Payment PLUS Venmo & Cash App
Venmo Address @FreebirdPublishers   Cash App Address #FreebirdPublishers

HOW TO *Keep it Interesting!*

MAIL-TAG

Mail-tag consists of an exchange of postal correspondence between two people. The first person begins the game by requesting one or more desired things. That person then mails those requests to the other participant - who interprets those requests, writes a list of their own requests for the other participant and sends them back. You can take as much or as little time to compose and send back your reply, ask for a few or as many things in your requests and generally interpret requests in whichever way you see fit.

Basically, you just write some questions or prompts out and enclose them with your letter. It's an easy way to remind yourself that an exchange should be a two-way conversation. I tend to be bad at this so this allows me to give my receipient something to, well, respond to.

LETTER GAME

A letter game involves the exchange of written letters between two or more participants. The first player writes a letter in the voice of a newly created character; in this first letter, the writer should establish her own identity and that of her correspondent, should set the scene, and should explain why she and her correspondent must communicate in written fashion. In subsequent letters, plot and character can be developed, but the writers should not talk about plot outside of the letters and the characters should never meet.

There are actual novels that were written using or inpired by this type of letter game, they include *Sorcery and Cecelia* or *The Enchanted Chocolate Pot*, *The Grand Tour* or *The Purloined Coronation Regalia*, and *The Mislaid Magician* or *Ten Years After*, all three by Patricia Wrede and Caroline Stevermer; *Freedom and Necessity*, by Steven Brust and Emma Bull; and the children's books *P.S. Longer Letter Later* and *Snail Mail No More* by Paula Danziger and Ann M. Martin.

Keep in mind when playing this "game" you are creating a new character, not yourself. Have fun with it and who knows...it could be the next number one selling novel! ;)

OPEN WHEN...

If you have some extra envelopes you can stand to part with, this next idea is a great one to put a smile on your pen pals face (whenever it's needed...not just the day they receive this package).

Write a letter for each of the following and place it in an envelope with the appropriate label. This gives your pen pal the opportunity to open the letter when they are feeling a certain way.

Example: Open when you have a bad day. When your pen pal is feeling down they can open your letter at that very moment in hopes of reading your letter and putting a smile on their face. This helps the two of you become more connected. You can actually be there for your freind in their time of need.

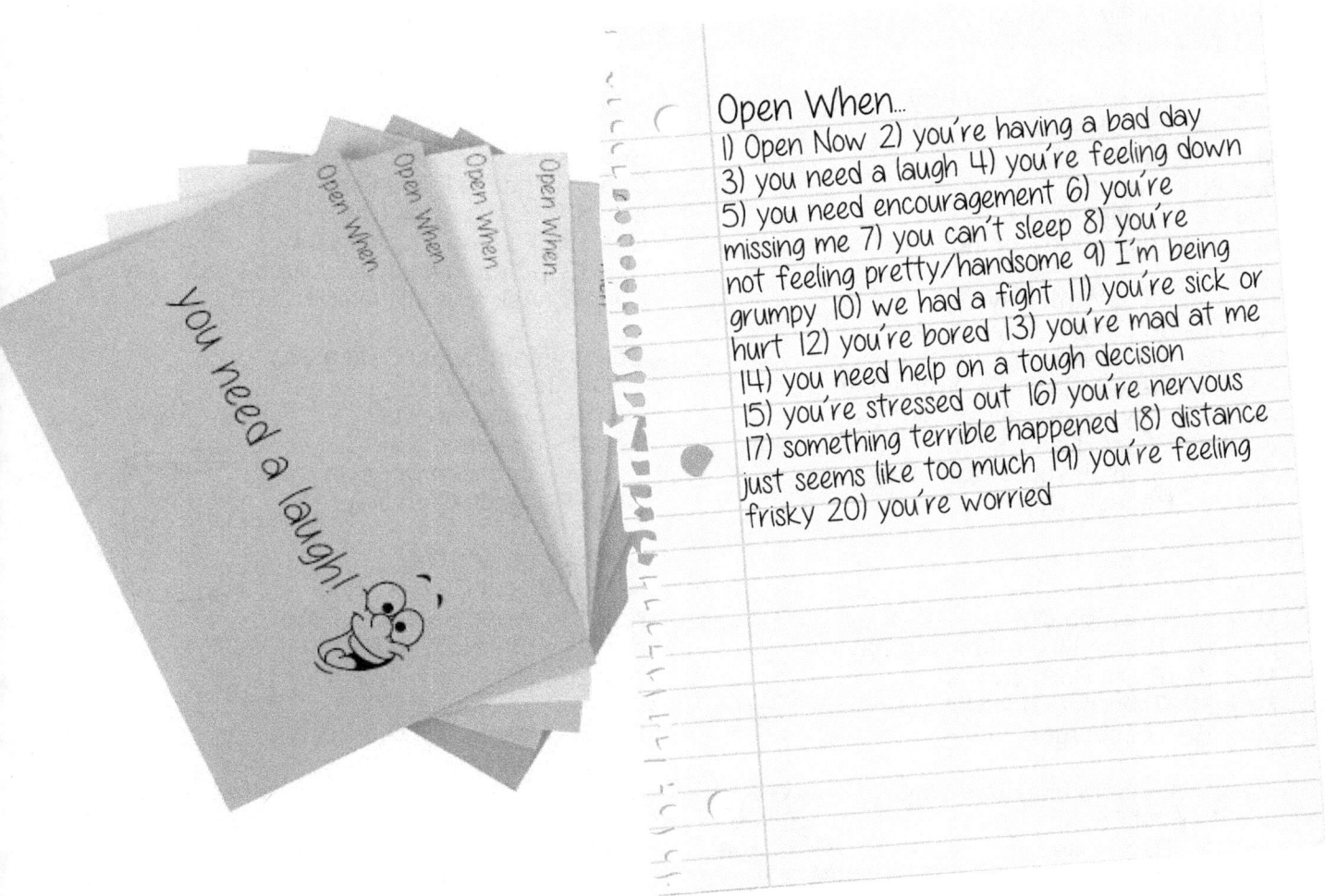

Open When...
1) Open Now 2) you're having a bad day 3) you need a laugh 4) you're feeling down 5) you need encouragement 6) you're missing me 7) you can't sleep 8) you're not feeling pretty/handsome 9) I'm being grumpy 10) we had a fight 11) you're sick or hurt 12) you're bored 13) you're mad at me 14) you need help on a tough decision 15) you're stressed out 16) you're nervous 17) something terrible happened 18) distance just seems like too much 19) you're feeling frisky 20) you're worried

HOW TO *Keep it Interesting!*

Did you know that today is National Donut Day? Not really...unless you're reading this on the first Friday in June or November 5th. Yeah, Donut Day has two different days of recognition. Sometimes the crazy Nationally recognized days can be good conversation starters. Here's some fun days.

Jan 1 - Polar Bear Plunge Day
Jan 4 - Trivia Day
Jan 9 - Clean Off Your Desk Day
Jan 14 - Organize Your Home Day
Jan 23 - Handwriting Day
Jan 27 - Chocolate Cake Day
Jan 31 - Backwards Day

Feb 1 - Work Naked Day
Feb 7 - Send a Card to a Friend Day
Feb 16 - Do a Grouch a Favor Day
Feb 24 - Tortilla Chip Day
Feb 28 - No Sleeping Day

Mar 1 - World Compliment Day
Mar 4 - High Five a Steve Day
Mar 13 - Napping Day
Mar 20 - Proposal Day
Mar 25 - Waffle Day
Mar 30 - Take a Walk in the Park Day

Apr 1 - Fun at Work Day
Apr 11 - Be Kind to Lawyers Day
Apr 13 - Scrabble Day
Apr 16 - Wear Pajamas to Work Day
Apr 22 - Jelly Bean Day
Apr 26 - Pretzel Day
Apr 27 - Poem in your Pocket Day
Apr 30 - Honesty Day

May 1 - Batman Day
May 4 - Star Wars Day
May 6 - Beverage Day
May 14 - Dance Like a Chicken Day
May 19 - Pizza Party Day
May 21 - Talk Like Yoda Day
May 28 - Hamburger Day

Jun 1 - Say Somthing Nice Day
Jun 8 - Best Friends Day
Jun 12 - Red Rose Day
Jun 18 - International Panic Day
Jun 23 - Typewriter Day

Jul 1 - International Joke Day
Jul 2 - I Forgot Day

Jul 6 - World Kissing Day
Jul 9 - Sugar Cookie Day
Jul 16 - Ice Cream Day
Jul 19 - Stick Out Your Tongue Day
Jul 23 - Vanilla Ice Cream Day
Jul 30 - National Cheesecake Day

Aug 1 - Girlfriend's Day
Aug 2 - Ice Cream Sandwich Day
Aug 4 - International Beer Day
Aug 9 - Book Lovers Day
Aug 13 - Left-Handers Day
Aug 16 - Tell A Joke Day
Aug 25 - Kiss and Make Up Day
Aug 31 - Eat Outside Day

Sep 4 - Eat an Extra Dessert Day
Sep 5 - Cheese Pizza Day
Sep 6 - Read a Book Day
Sep 13 - Positive Thinking Day
Sep 19 - International Talk Like a Pirate Day
Sep 28 - Ask a Stupid Question Day

Oct 1 - International Coffee Day
Oct 4 - Taco Day
Oct 16 - Dictionary Day
Oct 21 - Sweetest Day
Oct 27 - American Beer Day
Oct 30 - Candy Corn Day

Nov 1 - Author's Day
Nov 5 - Donut Day
Nov 13 - World Kindness Day
Nov 24 - Buy Nothing Day
Nov 26 - Cake Day

Dec 3 - Make a Gift Day
Dec 9 - Christmas Card Day
Dec 15 - Free Shipping Day (too bad the US Postal Service doesn't recognize this day. It's a day that larger retail stores offer free shipping which will guarantee your gifts arrive in time for Christmas.
Dec 19 - Ugly Sweater Day
Dec 26 - Thank You Note Day
Dec 31 - Make Up Your Mind Day

HOW TO *Keep it Interesting!*

MESSAGES THROUGH STAMPS

The messages of love through stamp placement started in the Victorian era when young lovers had to be careful about what they wrote and in getting their message across to their sweethearts. Some of those who have significant others serving overseas still use it. It has different meanings for different people but here's the most common.

Upside down: I love you.
Sideways, head right: Love and kisses.
Sideways, head left: I'll never leave you.
Diagonal to the right: Marry me?
Diagonal to the left: Yes, I'll marry you.

Just remember to always put the stamp in the upper right hand corner of your envelope regardless.

Postage Facts

- The first American post offices were located in taverns. When you needed to send a letter, you could stop by the local tavern and drop it in a special bag hanging for postal delivery.

- Stamps were not always sticky. Today when you place a stamp on an envelope, it comes with adhesive. Historically, stamps required you to use paste to stick it to a letter. Some even sewed stamps to the envelope.

- The forever stamp was first indroduced in 2007. This was a picture of a Liberty Bell and will always be worth the value of the current first class stamp, regardless of rate increases.

HOW TO *Keep it Interesting!*

There are several games that can be played through the mail. If you and your pen pal are looking for a little extra something to keep it entertaining then maybe mail game play is for you. Here are some ideas.

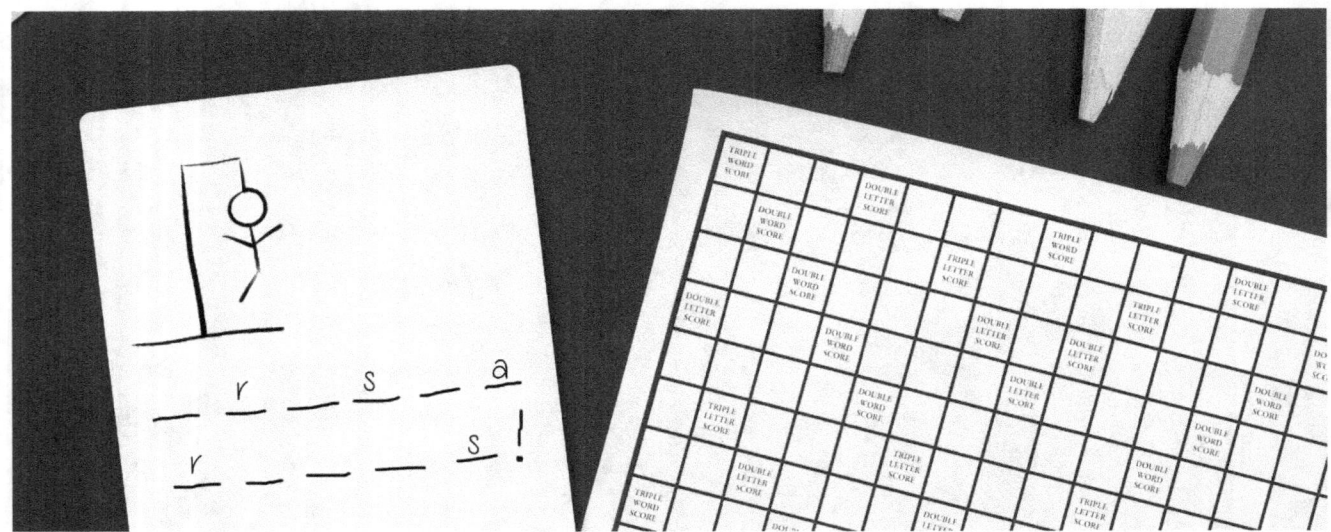

HANGMAN
This is an easy game that anyone will know how to play. Draw a little picture of a hangman's noose on a piece of paper to pass back and forth with your friend. However, make sure you write the solution to the puzzle down in a safe place so you don't forget the final message. To make opening the paper more exciting each time, add a little decoration or character around the edges of the game. At the end of the puzzle, you'll have a unique piece of art to remind you or your friend the fun time you had playing the game.

SCRABBLE
A little more intense than hangman, but you can play scrabble just as easily. Draw out a scrabble board on a sheet of paper with squares big enough to fit the letters. This game works best if you're willing to keep a scrabble board and pieces out for reference. You can play the game with your pen pal by sending them a slip of paper containing the letters they can use along with the sketch of the board. Have the person write the word they want to play on the paper board, and cross off the letters they used. When you receive the letter containing the game, remove those pieces from the person's stand and give them new ones, marking them down on a slip of paper. Then, play your own word and note it on the board. Keep repeating these steps until the game is over.

CHESS
You might be surprised to know that The United States Chess Federation actually has a page on their website dedicated to explaining the rules of correspondence chess. You can actually join and compete in tournaments, however if you want to just play with a pen pal, what you'll need is a chess board to mark each players turn and an agreement on how you'll be relaying the moves. Usually, chess players use algebraic notations, but you don't have to do this.

After you know who will be white or black, start sending moves. Continue this way until the game has ended. A game like this doesn't take up much space to note a new piece position. You may also want to draw out a board each time. I suggest two actually. One with the current board, the second with your new move. Then your opponent can do the same.

HOW TO *Keep it Interesting!*

BATTLESHIP

Draw out two 10 x 10 grids, labelled along the sides with letters and numbers. On the left-hand grid draw the rectangles representing your fleet of ships. Each fleet consists of the following ships:

1 x Aircraft Carrier - 5 squares
1 x Battleship - 4 squares
1 x Cruiser - 3 squares
2 x Destroyers - 2 squares each
2 x Submarines - 1 square each

During play the only thing that is exchanged is coordinates. When you receive a coordinate from your opponent you must tell them if it's a hit or a miss. When ships are completely hit you tell your opponent it's sunk. Keep going until one player has sunk all ships.

DOTS AND BOXES

Take turns with your pen pal drawing lines between dots on a grid. You can do as small or as large of a grid as you'd like. Each player should use a different color. The opponent who closes each box gets to write his/her initials inside the box. The player who completes the most boxes wins.

The game is more complex than it initially appears, and even on a small grid there is plenty of opportunity for skilful play.

Tweak these games to make them your own and personalize them for your pen pals. Try coming up with your own game ideas as well. Think about all of the old games you played using a pencil and paper when you were a kid (like tic tac toe). You might be surprised by what you can play through the mail.

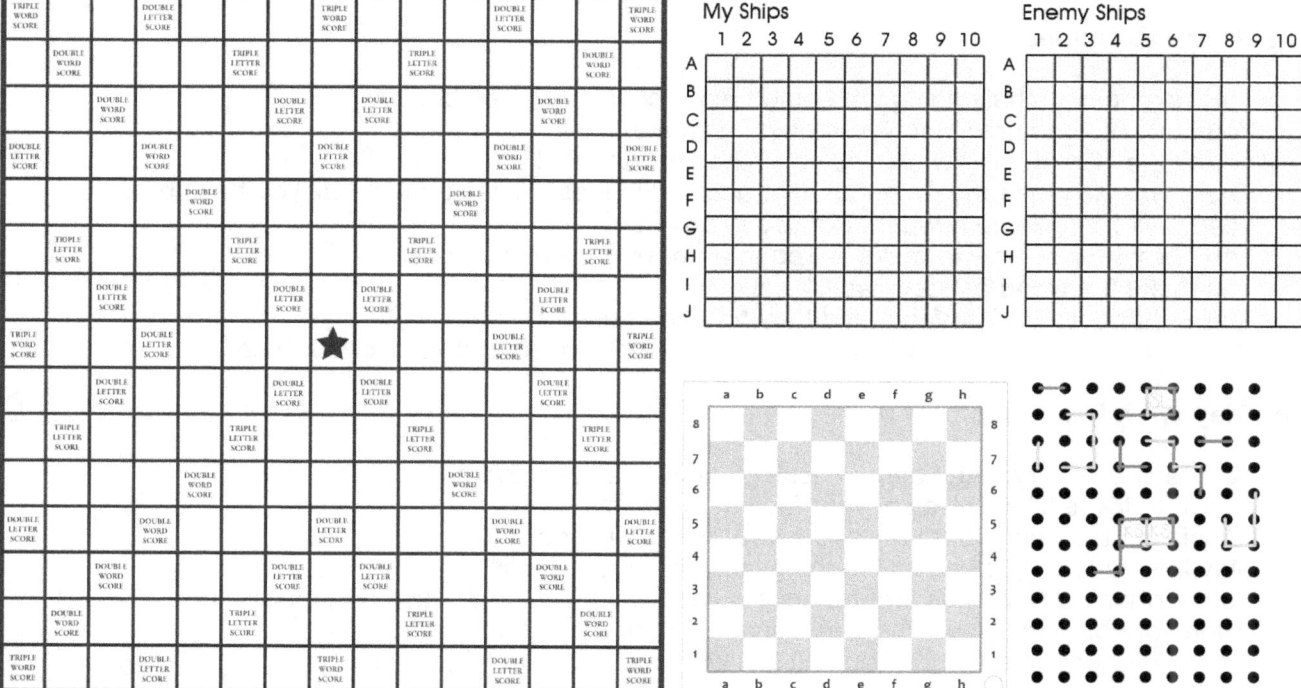

Pen Pals: A Personal Guide for Prisoners

33

HOW TO *Find the Right Words*

We all need a little help finding the right words sometimes. From the need to find a good way to wish someone a Happy Birthday to sharing our condolences over the loss of a loved one or friend. Here's some examples to put you on the right path. Remember, it's always good to elaborate on these and add a personal touch as well.

Thank You Examples:

- "This has been a challenging time, and I appreciate you so much."
- "You have no idea how much your help has meant."
- "For all the little and big ways you've pitched in…thanks!"
- "There was nothing random about your acts of kindness. Thank you for all you have done."
- "I can never thank you enough. But this is a start."
- "You always know how to make life brighter for everyone you know."
- "You make the world a nicer place."
- "You went above and beyond, and I am touched and grateful."
- "You took common courtesy to an uncommon level. I'm so grateful for your help."

Birthday Wish Examples:

- "You deserve everything happy. Wishing you that all year long!"
- "I hope today is filled will all of your favorite guilty pleasures."
- "Wishing you a happy birthday and a year that's blessed."
- "May this day bring to you all the things that make you smile."
- "Your birthday only comes around once a year - make it count, have an amazing day."
- "Hope your birthday is just the beginning of a year full of happiness."
- "Happy Birthday to a friend I couldn't live without!"

- "In case I don't tell you often enough, I really appreciate your frienship. And I'm so grateful for all you bring into my life!"
- "This getting older stuff isn't for sissies. Glad I have a friend like you to go first!"
- "Love you, my sweet friend. Happy Birthday."

Get Well Examples:

- "Hope you get to feeling better soon."
- "Wishing you well."
- "Sending good, healthy vibes your way."
- "Warmest wishes for a speedy recovery!"
- "Hope you're feeling a little better every day."
- "You're in my warmest thoughts as you recover."
- "You mean so much to me. Hope you're feeling better very soon."
- "I don't know what to say, except I love you and I'm thinking of you. Get well soon!"

Terminal Illness Examples:

- "Thinking about you every day."
- "Thoughts of you are always some of my happiest. Always will be."
- "In my heart and in my prayers. Always...especially now."
- "I'm praying for a miricle cure, hey it doesn't hurt to ask."
- "Just wanted to remind you how important you are to me."
- "Hope you feel all the love surrounding you right now."

Sympathy Examples:

- "Sharing in your sadness as you remember [name]."
- "Sending healing prayers and comforting hugs I'm so sorry for your loss."
- "I was saddened to hear about the passing of [name or relationship]. My thoughts are with you and your family during this tough time."
- "Thinking of you and wishing you moments of peace and comfort as you remember a friend who was so close to you."
- "Holding you close in my thoughts and hoping you are doing okay."
- "What an amazing person and what a remarkable life. I feel so lucky that I got to know him/her."
- "Your [relationship] was an amazing person. I feel priviledged to have known him/her. I know you will miss him/her deeply. I'll be keeping you in my thoughts and prayers."

Anniversary Examples:

- "Wishing a perfect pair a perfectly happy day."
- "Here's to another year of being great together."
- "Always knew the two of you had something special."
- "Another year, another great reason to celebrate."
- "Hope you find the time to look back on all of your sweet memories together."

Anniversary to Partner/Spouse Examples:

- "I'm so lucky to have your and your love. Thanks for putting up with me for another year."
- "So grateful that God gave me you to love."
- "I never dreamed that love could be this good."
- "Every day I still discover new things about you to love."
- "It's been a tough year, but our lough is tougher. Thanks for staying strong through it all. Here's to us and a brighter year ahead."

HOW TO *Improve Your Handwriting*

from *illegible* to incredible!

Part 1: Analyze Your Handwriting

1. Write a paragraph. Choose a topic—anything really—and write at least five sentences about it. If you're not feeling too creative, simply copy a passage out of a book or newspaper. The goal is to get an idea of what your handwriting looks like on average. The more you write, the more accurate your analysis will be.

2. Identify the primary shapes. Is your handwriting full of loops and curves? Is it straight and stiff in appearance? Do you have hard corners, or do your letters blend together?

3. Look for a slant. The angle you write your letters can make or break your handwriting. Is your handwriting perpendicular to the lines under it? Does it fall to the left or to the right significantly? A slight slant is typically not a problem, but too much of a slant can make it difficult for someone else to read.

4. Pay attention to your alignment. Do your words tend to be written on an upwards or downwards angle? Do they overlap with the lines on the page? Is every word individually angeled or do your entire lines of text head in a similar direction away from the line?

5. Look at the spacing. The distance between your words and letters helps determine the quality of your handwriting. There should be enough space between each word to fit the letter "O". Using more or less space than this can be an indicator of poor handwriting. Pay attention also to the closeness of each individual letter. Cramped writing or letters that are spaced far apart are also difficult to read.

6. Pay attention to the size. Turns out size does matter (at least when it comes to handwriting). Does your writing fill up the entire space between the two lines? Taking up a large amount of space or using too little are both things to avoid.

7. Analyze your line quality. look at the actual lines that comprise your writing. Are they drawn with heavy pressure, or are they faint and hard to read? Are your lines straight, or are they kind of squiggly and uneven?

8. Determine your flaws. Considering all of the aforementioned, what is it that your handwriting needs in order to improve? Possible changes can be made to the shape of letters, your spacing, alignment, writing size, line quality, and the slant of words. Changing one or more of these will improve your overall handwriging legibility.

Part 2: Changing Your Handwriting

1. Write in the air. Most of the time, people with poor or illegible handwriting simply haven't properly trained the correct muscle groups in their hands, arms, and shoulders. Avoid "drawing" letters with your hand, and instead write by moving your entire arm up to the shoulder. To practice doing this, the easiest thing is to write sentences in the air using your finger. This forces you to use the muscle groups in your arm and shoulder that help to improve handwriting and keep it from looking messy or cramped.

2. Adjust the shape of your hand. Your pen or pencil should be held between your thumb and index and (optional) middle fingers. The end of the writing utensil should rest against either the web of your hand or against the knuckle of your index finger. Holding your pencil too tightly or loosely (in this position or others) will result in poor handwriting. Hold the pencil in the bottom ⅓ for the best results.

3. Practice the basic shapes. A consistent flaw in poor handwriting is irregularity and inconsistency between letters and shapes. All the letters are made up out of straight lines and circles or semi-circles, so put in some time drawing these. Fill an entire sheet of paper with parallel vertical lines, and parallel diagonal lines. Do the same with a sheet of 'o' shapes as well. When you can consistently make the same line over and over, you are ready to move onto complete letters.

4. Study a directional chart. Although everyone seems to do it a bit differently, there is a certain way to write each letter of the alphabet. Following the correct direction of the line that forms each letter can greatly improve your handwriting. For example, rather than starting a lowercase 'a' with the tail, begin at the top of the loop. Practice writing every letter in the correct direction, just like how you were taught in kindergarten.

5. Try a variety of writing utensils. Although it may seem nit-picky, different people are able to write better (or worse!) using different writing utensils. Try a variety of tools including a ballpoint, roll-on, and felt pen in addition to traditional and mechanical pencils. Finding one that you enjoy writing with may be enough to improve your handwriting on its own.

6. Practice your alphabet. Yes, just like in first grade, fill up rows upon rows of lines with each letter of the alphabet in lower and uppercase. Use your font inspiration that you gathered as well as your handwriting analysis to focus on what you need to change. If slanting is your problem, make it a point to keep your letters vertical. If you are trying to change the shapes of your letters, concentrate simulating the shapes you see in the handwriting inspiration you've chosen.

7. Get it down pat. When you're certain of your every letter's perfection, practice writing them in full words and sentences. Write the phrase "the quick brown fox jumps over the lazy dog" over and over again—this particular sentence contains every letter of the alphabet, giving you ample practice time. Although it may seem monotonous, the adage 'practice makes perfect' certainly applies here.

Reprinted from http://www.wikihow.com/Improve-Your-Handwriting

HOW TO *Be More Descriptive*

Descriptive words basically help to paint a picture in your pen pal's head. So be sure to choose wisely. Instead of saying nice, good, say, pretty, etc we can choose to use more powerful words that mean the same thing but envoke a more detailed view.

INSTEAD OF SAID:
called	shouted
cried	whispered
responded	remarked
demanded	questioned
asked	replied
stated	exclaimed

INSTEAD OF LAUGHED:
snickered	guffawed
giggled	cackled
roared	howled
chuckled	tittered
crowed	bellowed
chortled	shrieked

INSTEAD OF RAN:
hurried	bolted
raced	darted
scurried	sped
dashed	jogged
galloped	sprinted
trotted	rushed

INSTEAD OF WALKED:
staggered	shuffled
traveled	sauntered
trudged	lumbered
strutted	paraded
marched	ambled
hiked	strolled

INSTEAD OF SAW:
glimpsed	glanced at
noticed	eyed
observed	gazed at
sighted	spied
spotted	examined
stared at	watched

INSTEAD OF LIKE:
love	prefer
admire	cherish
appreciate	care for
fancy	favor
adore	enjoy
idolize	treasure

INSTEAD OF SAD:
downcast	unhappy
depressed	dejected
woeful	forlorn
gloomy	melancholy
miserable	crestfallen
sorrowful	mournful

INSTEAD OF PRETTY:
beautiful	exquisite
lovely	gorgeous
glamorous	stunning
attractive	handsome
elegant	striking
cute	fair

INSTEAD OF GOOD:
great	splendid
pleasant	superb
marvelous	grand
delightful	terrific
superior	amazing
wonderful	excellent

INSTEAD OF LITTLE:
teeny	small
diminutive	tiny
compact	minuscule
microscopic	miniature
petite	slight
wee	minute

INSTEAD OF NICE:
kind	congenial
benevolent	agreeable
thoughtful	courteous
gracious	warm
considerate	cordial
decent	humane

INSTEAD OF FUNNY:
farcical	hysterical
jocular	sidesplitting
amusing	hilarious
humorous	laughable
witty	silly
comical	nonsensical

INSTEAD OF BIG:		INSTEAD OF HAPPY:		INSTEAD OF GOOD:	
towering	enormous	glad	merry	witty	ingenious
huge	tremendous	jovial	contented	bright	sharp
large	massive	jubilant	pleased	quick-witted	brainy
great	giant	joyful	delighted	knowledgeable	brilliant
gigantic	colossal	thrilled	jolly	intelligent	gifted
mammoth	immense	cheerful	elated	clever	wise

ROMANTIC *Words to Use*

Because you may want to elicit a romantic relationship with your new pen pal...here are some words you may want to use (more on writing a love letter later).

A - adorable, alluring, angel, awesome, attractive, amazing

B - babe, baby, beautiful, bedazzled, beloved, bewitching, beauty, blessing, breathtaking

C - charming, cute, classy, ,cookie, cuddly, clever, cutie pie, captivating, complete me

D - dear, darling, dazzling, delightful, delectable, delicious, divine, doll, desire, devotion, dearest.

E - elegant, enchanting, endearing, exciting, extraordinary, exceptional, everything (as in you're my everything)

F - fabulous, fascinating, feminine, friend, foxy, forgiving, fun, funny, fantasy

G - gorgeous, grand, great, generous, gifted, giving, gracious, genuine

H - heavenly, hot, hot stuff, heart's desire, hunk, helpful, huggable

I - incomparable, immortal, intimate, irreplaceable, inspirational, intoxicating, inspiring

J - joyful, joyous

K - kissable, kinky

L - love of my life, light of my life, love bug, lover, luscious, lustful, long for, lovable, loving

M - magnetic, magnificent, marvelous, mellow, mesmerizing, moving, my everything

N - nasty, naughty, nurturing

O - (the) one, (my) only, outrageous, one of a kind, open-minded,

P - passionate, partner, perfect, precious, pretty, playmate, playful, provacative

Q - queen, quick-witted, quality

R - radiant, ravishing, red-hot, remarkable, revel, revere, romantic, rose

S - sassy, seductive, sensual, sexual, smart, sexy, scruptious, sinful, spicy, sweet, sunshine, sugar, sweetheart

T - tantalizing, tasty, tease, tender, titilate, tempt treasure, true love, talented, thoughtful

U - unforgettable, unique, unselfish, upbeat, understanding

V - vibrant, vixen, value, virtuous, vulnerable

W - warm, wild, winsome, wonderful, woman, worship, warm-hearted, well-mannered, wise, witty, wonderful

X - x-rated

Y - you, yummy

Z - zaftig, zazzy, zesty

HOW TO Start & Close Your Letters

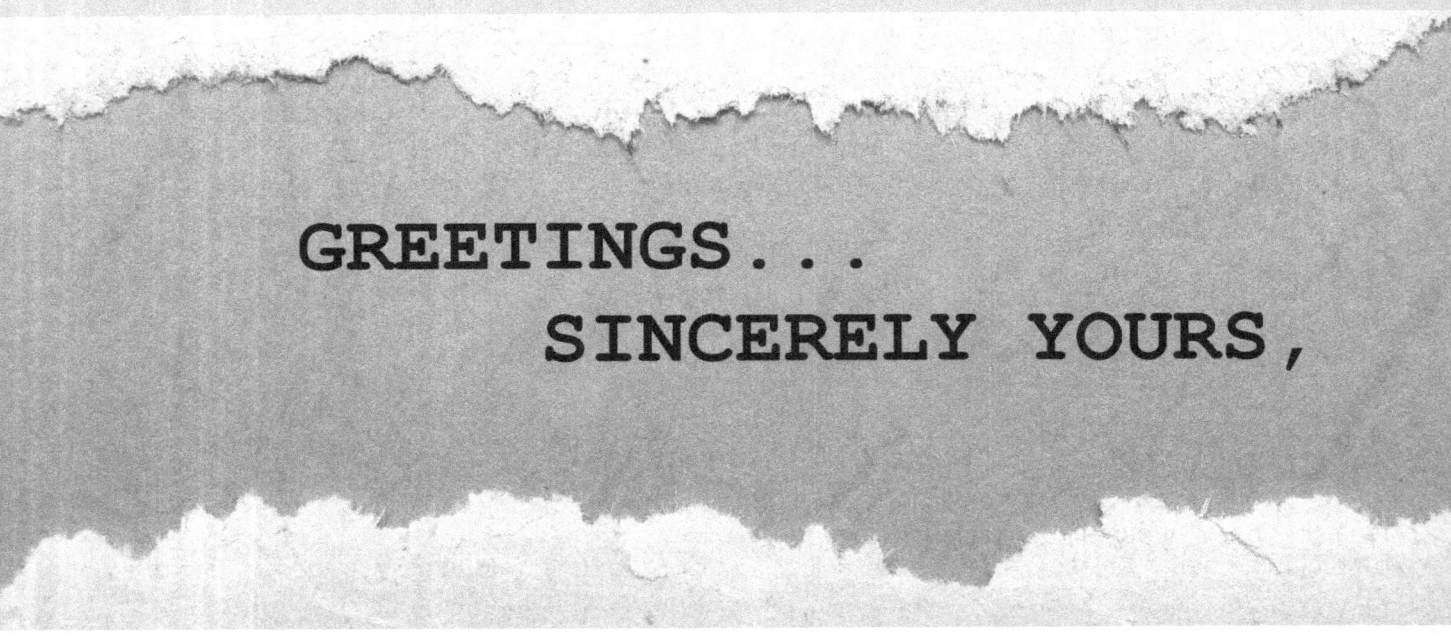

The current traditional way of addressing someone in a friendly letter is "Dear" and closing such letter "Sincerely" but there are alot of other ways to do so if you want to get a little more creative. Here are some options for both informal and formal greetings and closings.

Formal Greetings

- Dear
- Dearest
- Greetings

Informal Greetings

- Greetings and Salutations
- Hello
- Hey there
- Hi
- Hi-hey-hello
- How's it going?
- What are you up to?
- What's going on?
- What's Happenin?
- What's New?
- What's Up?

Formal Closings

- Best Regards
- Kind Regards
- Many Thanks
- Regards
- Respectfully
- Respectfully Yours
- Sincerely
- Sincerely Yours
- Thanks
- Thank You
- Thank you for your consideration
- Truly Yours
- Yours Cordially
- Yours Respectfully
- Yours Sincerely

Informal Closings

Sweet Letter Closings

- Always in my thoughts
- Be Safe, Be Healthy, Be Happy
- Be Well
- Blessings
- Cordially
- Health and happiness
- Kindly
- Peace and Progress
- Truly
- Until Next Time

Fun Letter Endings

- Be good or be good at it
- Bottoms up
- Buh bye
- Catch you on the next bounce
- Cheers Big Ears
- Chow Mein
- From the mind of a genius
- Full of hot air
- Get it? Got it? Good.
- I need some closure
- Later Tater
- Later Vader
- Love, Peace, and Chicken Grease
- Made in America
- Marking my spot
- Scratch and Sniff
- See ya round like a donut
- Smell ya later
- Tag, your it
- Take care, comb your hair
- The man of steel
- There can only be one
- This message will self distruct
- Toodles
- Over and Out

Love Letter Endings

- Adoringly Yours
- Affectionately
- Always
- Always by your side
- Always & Forever
- Always, forever...plus a day
- Always in my thoughts
- Devoted to you
- Eternally Yours
- Hopelessly in Love
- Love
- Love to love you
- Love you madly, need you badly, miss you sadly
- Love you now and forever
- Love you so much
- LYLC = Love You Like Crazy
- Missing You
- Missing you with every breath
- My heart is forever yours
- Till death do us part
- Truly
- With kind affection
- Words aren't enough
- XOXO
- Yearning for You
- You are always in my thoughts and I don't mind
- Your #1 Fan
- Yours ever
- Yours faithfully
- Yours regardless

P.S. MESSAGES *Just for Laughs*

P.S. Look Behind You
P.S. Never take life seriously. No one gets out alive anyway.
P.S. I love you so much if my nose was running money I would blow it all on you.
P.S. If you were a booger, I'd pick you.
P.S. Just remember if we get caught, you're deaf and I don't speak English
P.S. If being awesome was a crime, I'd be serving life.
P.S. I don't have a dirty mind, I have a sexy imagination.
P.S. Its okay if you disagree with me. I can't force you to be right.
P.S. I am putting you on my "to-do" list.
P.S. Sometimes I pretend to be normal, but it gets boring so I go back to being me.
P.S. Life is short. Smile while you still have teeth.
P.S. Life always offers you a second chance, it's called tomorrow.
P.S. I hate it when i'm singing a song and the artist gets the words wrong.
P.S. If you say "gullible" slowly it sounds like "oranges"

HOW TO *Write a Love Letter*

Get over your fears. You're in control of what you write or don't write. You don't have to follow some love letter template or write poetry or sappy phrases unless you want to. The best thing you can do is be yourself in your letter. It will go much further than attempting to say things that you're significant other (or potential significant other) knows doesn't sound like you. They're talking to you for a reason. They like YOU.

Writing a love letter is a perfect opportunity for you to open up and be transparent about your feelings. You are digging deep into your emotions as you put yourself out there. Let your emotions flow onto each sheet of paper. These words are an extension of you and your feelings for your lover.

Avoid being too casual, too light-hearted, or openly erotic. A love letter is a letter of respect that conveys deep, difficult to express feelings. Be real. Your love letter should be a carefully crafted work of sincere art. Be confident as you express your emotions, dreams, and vulnerability.

It's easiest if you have some ideas when writing a love letter and the easier it is the more you'll be able to write and the more often you'll wish to do so. As in most tasks the first thing to do is to brainstorm. Just grab a sheet of paper and start jotting some topics, attributes, or feelings simply put. For example: Smile/Eyes, Sexy Body, Generous Spirit, Sexy Talk, Time apart, Willingness to overlook the past, future goals together. There is no right or wrong here (also see love letter ideas on next page).

Make your significant other feel it from the start by choosing a sweet salutation.

- ♥ My dearest darling
- ♥ My love
- ♥ My soulmate
- ♥ To the love of my life

Mention why you're writing.

- ♥ I wanted to wish you a Happy Valentine's Day
- ♥ I just felt like telling you...
- ♥ Because I wanted to share my love with you

See the future.

- ♥ What are you looking forward to together?
- ♥ Seeing him/her on an upcoming visit?
- ♥ Still loving each other when you're old and gray?

Be descriptive.

- ♥ Your smile is like the sun rising and brings a new day to my life.
- ♥ My heart leaps like a hummingbird in flight everytime I see you.
- ♥ Sometimes I think my heart will burst with all of the longing and excitement I feel when I think of you.

Finish Strong.

- ♥ All my love
- ♥ Forever yours
- ♥ Tenderly
- ♥ Your loving (wife, husband, girlfriend, boyfriend)

Love Letter Ideas/Prompts

- ♥ How much you love him/her
- ♥ What you felt the first time you met or exchanged letters
- ♥ What you love about him/her
- ♥ A list of compliments
- ♥ Write him/her a poem
- ♥ Draw a picture that illustrates your relationship
- ♥ List relationship goals you've achieved
- ♥ List relationship goals you wish to accomplish
- ♥ Share dreams of your future
- ♥ List of why you are proud of him/her
- ♥ Why you couldn't live without them
- ♥ Dream of a trip you'd love to take with him/her
- ♥ Tell them how in love you are at this very moment
- ♥ Write about a specific attribute that you love about them-such as her kindness
- ♥ Send them lyrics to your favorite song or a song that makes you think of them
- ♥ Share what you love about your relationship in the past, present, future
- ♥ Recap a particularly pleasant day you spent together or a phone conversation you cherished
- ♥ Let them know how positively different your life is now that you have each other.

PENPAL
Sites for Prisoners

PENPAL SITES *for Prisoners*

💰 = Costs to Join
💵 = Free to Join
⭐ = Highly Rated

BLACK AND PINK 💵
Self-proclaimed radical anti-establishment, anti-capitalism, gay liberation organization started in Boston. Has monthly prisoner newspaper.
Pen pal matching site - they match LGBTQIA2S+ persons with someone safe to write. Pen pal listings NOT the primary focus.

Address:
Black and Pink
614 Columbia Rd.
Dorchester, MA 02125

Website: blackandpink.org
Cost: Free to Join

CAGED LADIES 💰
Ladies only, sorry guys. If you're a woman seeking a pen pal you can be listed on their site for $15/year. They do not accept checks or money orders. Payments and listings are only done through their website.

Address:
No mailing address listed.

Website: cagedladies.com
Cost: $15/year

CONPALS INMATE CONNECTIONS ⭐💰
Several profile types available: Personal, Legal, Art/Business. Basic profile is $50. They also offer person e-mail accounts with weekly emailing starting at $45/year.

Address:
Conpals Inmate Connections
465 NE 181st Ave #308
Portland, OR 97230

Website: convictpenpals.com
Cost: Starting at $50/year

FORGOTTEN FEMALES 💵
Their efforts are to assist women in prison in having a voice and being heard. Their profiles are free and encourage you to tell your story in hopes of being heard. Accepts no photos. Profiles can be up to 150 words.

Address:
Forgotten Females
C/O Mc Lloyd Services
Box 3621
Wichita, KS 67201

Website: http://forgottenfemales.tripod.com
Cost: Free

PENPAL SITES *for Prisoners*

💰 = Costs to Join
💲 = Free to Join
⭐ = Highly Rated

FRIENDS BEYOND THE WALL 💰 ⭐
Connecting members with the outside world since 1999. They offer premium pen pal services. Profiles starting at $39.95 include 250 words and a photo. Legal profiles are also available. Website is easy to navigate and possesses a search feature to narrow down results.

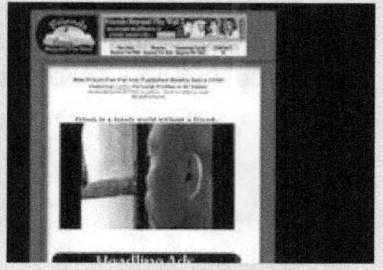

Address:
Friends Beyond the Wall, Inc.
55 Mansion St #1030
Poughkeepsie, NY 12602

Website: friendsbeyondthewall.com
Cost: $29.95/6 months, $39.95/year, $59.95/2years

GOOD PRISONER 💰
GoodPrisoner is a listing of male only prisoners who are looking for positive connections with those from the outside. They provide a year plus pen pal page for a price (which is not mentioned on the site). Contact them for a brochure. GoodPrisoner has a sister site for female inmates, femaleprisonerpals.com.

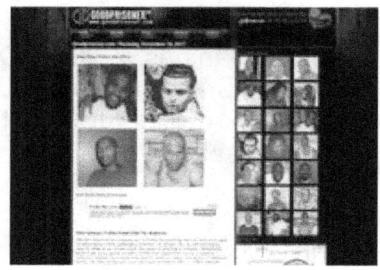

Address:
GoodPrisoner
Box 12
Buffalo, NY 14215-0012

Website: goodprisoner.com
Cost: Paid Profiles, Cost Unavailable

HOT PRISON PALS 💰
Website objective is to bring people together who are looking for more than just a pen pal relationship. Hot Prison Pals aims to connect you to that soul mate. They also feature 7 hot inmates per week which address is only available through online donations by individuals interested.

Address:
Hot Prison Pals
373 Broadway Suite C-2
New York, N.Y. 10013

Website: hotprisomnpals.com
Cost: Starting at $19/year

INMATE CLASSIFIED ⭐ 💰
Founded in 1996, Inmate Classified was created to address inmates needs to reconnect with friends and family as well as facilitating positive communication with pen pals around the world. Profiles and packages ranging from $60-$200.

Address:
Inmate Classified
Box 3311
Granada Hills, CA 91394

Website: inmate.com
Cost: $60-$200

Pen Pals: A Personal Guide for Prisoners

PENPAL SITES *for Prisoners*

💰 = Costs to Join
💲 = Free to Join
★ = Highly Rated

INMATE-CONNECTION ★ 💰
Their mission is to attract sincere pen pals who can bring inmates love, friendship and happiness. They offer a $40 profile for a 2 year listing.

Address:
Inmate-Connection
Box 83987
Los Angeles, CA 90083

Website: inmate-connection.com
Cost: Use $40/2year

INMATE MINGLE 💰
New company as of 2017. Offers three levels of membership, Gallery $30, Gold $40, Platinum $50. Unique ability to add music to your page to show off your favorite song. Printable Brochures available online, or send SASE for brochure.

Address:
Inmate Mingle
Box 23207
Columbia, SC 29224

Website: inmatemingle.com
Cost: $30-$50

LOST VAULT 💲
Lost Vault is dedicated to maintaining a free place for inmates to find pen pals, and for people to find them. They do not accept free pen pal ads via snail mail except for death row inmates and they will be verified. For ads posted by their staff, there is a nominal $10 fee for all inmates other than death row, who receive free ads. Pen pal submissions cannot be accepted via e-mail, use their online form.

Address:
Lost Vault
Box 242
Mascot, TN 37806

Website: lostvault.com
Cost: Basic Ad $35, VIP $65

LOVEAPRISONER.COM 💰 ★
Their mission is to give inmates a sense of hopefulness by connecting them to the outside world. You can have up to 250 words and one photo in your ad. VIP services available.

Address:
Loveaprisoner.com
Box 192
Dequincy, LA 70633

Website: loveaprisoner.com
Cost: Basic Ad $35, VIP $65

PENPAL SITES *for Prisoners*

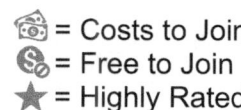
= Costs to Join
= Free to Join
= Highly Rated

MEET-AN-INMATE.COM
Membership application available on their website or send SASE for printed version. Featured Ads start at $70 and place a thumbnail photo on their home page. Regular Ad starts at $35.

Address:
Meet-An-Inmate.com
Attn: Arlen Bischke
Box 845
Winchester, OR 97495

Website: meet-an-inmate.com
Cost: Regular Ad $35, Featured Ad 70

PAPER DOLLS
Paper dolls is a pen pal site for women inmates. Services start at $10. Send SASE for Brochure/Application. Email service is available for people to write to you from your Paper Dolls profile for $5/month or $50/year for unlimited email. You can have to up 100 words and one photo in your ad.

Address:
Peper Dolls
Box 218
Oregon, WI 53575

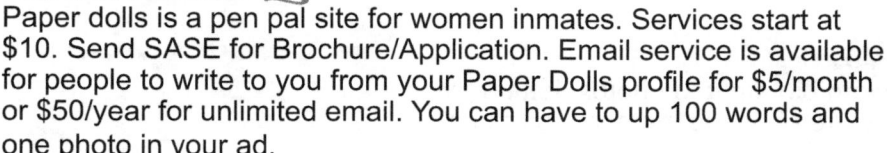
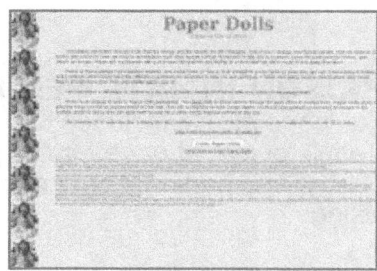

Website: paperdollspenpals.com
Cost: Starting at $10

PENACON
Penacon is recently under the ownership of Freebird Publishers, a leader among prisoner services. Dedicated to helping you gain connections Penacon advertises and networks to ensure maximum exposure of your profile. One year profile is $35 or $95 for the duration of your sentence. Offers premier profile listings for an additional $5/month which places you on the homepage.

Address:
Penacon
221 Pearl St., Ste. 533
North Dighton, MA 02764

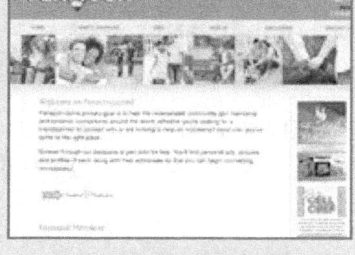

Website: penacon.com
Cost: $35/year or $95 Until Release

PRISON FRIENDSHIP
Will not accept members with any crimes against children. Profiles starting at $19.99/6 months, $39.99/year. Offer videograms and video messages on profiles. Institution checks, money orders, and cash app accepted.

Address:
Prison Friendship LLC
Box 24481
Dayton, OH 45424

Website: prisonfriendship.com
Cost: Starting at $19.99

Pen Pals: A Personal Guide for Prisoners

PENPAL SITES *for Prisoners*

💵 = Costs to Join
💲⃠ = Free to Join
★ = Highly Rated

PRISON INMATES ONLINE 💵
Serving inmates since 2000. They call their online service "Write to Prisoners Project". They sort their profiles by many categories including: male, female, gay, lesbian, bi-sexual, serving life, death row, needs mail, and by state. They'll also host inmates artwork, tattoos, photos, and classifieds. Send SASE for brochure. Inmate Profiles starting at $40.

Address:
Prison Inmates Online, LLC
8033 W Sunset Blvd. #7000
Los Angeles, CA 90046

Website: prisoninmates.com
Cost: $40

PRISON INMATE PEN PAL 💵
Full page profile includes 800 word bio, up to 3 photos, letters by e-mail, personal page for art, picture changes, personal page for poetry, and personal blog page. Profile listing costs $25 for 4 year listing.

Address:
Inmate Outreach Program
7765 Tigertail Rd Suite 1
Saint Pauls, NC 28384-8907

Website: prisoninmatepenpal.com
Cost: $25/4 years

PRISON PEN PALS 💵 ★
They offer five different types of ads: Economy, Basic, Gold Star, Platinum and Gallery. The prices start at $9.95 a year and go up to $99.95 a year. You can customize your ad package to get exactly what you need, such as background music and additional photos.

Address:
Prison Pen Pals
Box 235
East Berlin, PA 17316

Website: prisonpenpals.com
Cost: $9.95 - $99.95/year

SimpliMingle 💵 ★
Users can send text messages directly to your SimpliMingle number just like they would any other text message or call and leave voice messages. When you call the SimpliMingle number using voice activated commands you can navigate the menu, listen and send voice messages that are delivered to the persons mobile phone as an audio clip.

Address:
SimpliMingle
Box 147
Swansea, MA 02777

Website: simplimingle.com
Cost: Starting at $19.99/month

PENPAL SITES *for Prisoners*

💵 = Costs to Join
💲 = Free to Join
★ = Highly Rated

SURROGATE SISTERS 💵
Surrogate Sisters has been around for 11 years offering other by mail services to inmates. They have now expanded into the internet with pen pal profiles. They do not list prices on their site, send SASE for information.

Address:
Surrogate Sisters
Box 95043
Las Vegas, NV 89193

Website: surrogatesisters.com
Cost: Not Posted, Contact for Info

FRIENDS 4 PRISONERS 💵
At Friends 4 Prisoners, They pair inmates looking for a pen pal with non-incarcerated individuals who want to make a difference in someone else's life. One year memberships starting at $50/year.

Address:
Friends 4 Prisoners
20770 Hwy 281 N, Suite 108-178
San Antonio, TX 78258

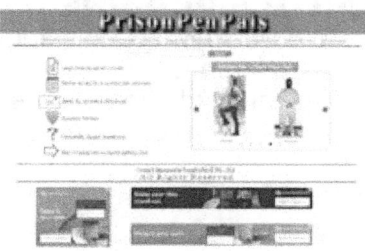

Website: friends4prisoners.com
Cost: $50+

WIRE OF HOPE 💵
Connecting incarcerated people with volunteer pen pals from all over the world for a meaningful experience. Profiles starting at $45/year. Ability to add a 30-second voice message, with two photos and a 350 word bio.

Address:
For those incarcerated in AL, AR, CT, DC, DE, FL, GA, IA, IL, IN, KY, LA, MA, MD, ME, MI, MO, MS, NC, NH, NJ, NY, OH, PA, RI, SC, TN, VA, VT, WV or in the US Commonwealth & Territories:

Wire of Hope
Box 7717
Jacksonville, FL 32238 • USA

For those incarcerated in AK, AZ, CA, CO, HI, ID, KS, MN, MT, ND, NE, NM, NV, OK, OR, SD, TX, UT, WA, WI, WY or outside the US:

Wire of Hope
2000 Vassar St. #10731
Reno, NV 89510 • USA

Website: wireofhope.com
Cost: $45+

PENPAL SITES *for Prisoners*

💰 = Costs to Join
💲 = Free to Join
★ = Highly Rated

WOMEN BEHIND BARS ★ 💰
Women Behind Bars has been interviewed by hundreds of radio stations and written up in hundreds of newspapers. The listing is free for women inmates and prospective pen pals pay a small fee of $4 per address. You can have up to 100 words and one photo in your ad. You will need an application.

Address:
Todd Muffoletto
Box 284
Hobart, IN 46342

Website: womenbehindbars.com
Cost: Free

WRITE A PRISONER 💰
Write A Prisoner is dedicated to positive changes for inmates. They offer standard ads for $65/year which include 250 words and a photo. Additional words and photos are available at an upgraded cost. They also offer blogs and poetry add ons.

Address:
Write A Prisoner
Box 10
Edgewater, FL 32132

Website: writeaprisoner.com
Cost: Starting at $65/year

INMATE SHOPPER

Looking for futher information, more directories and listings? Check out the Inmate Shopper.

1000+ Listings AMERICA'S LARGEST Resource for Inmate Services. Everything you need from the outside while in prison is available in this book. All new content in each issue, constantly updated with products, services, resources, news, sports schedules, sexy non nude photo spread, pen pal section and more. Softcover 8"x10". B&W, 325+ pages.

SEE THE FOLLOWING PAGE FOR MORE INFORMATION AND ORDERING DETAILS.

FREEBIRD PUBLISHERS

Pro Se Collection by Raymond E. Lumsden

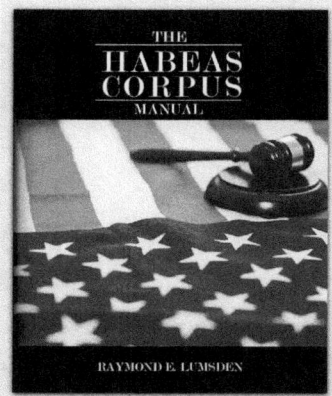

This legal collection is the no-nonsense, easy to understand, and effective work by one of Freebird Publisher's Best Selling Legal Authors, Raymond E. Lumsden. Specifically written by an inmate with extensive legal training and education, for inmates seeking relief in the twisting and confusing legal system of America.

★ Easy to follow instructions;
★ Dozens of sample motions and pleadings;
★ Up to date case citings and writings;
★ **5 Star Amazon Ratings;**
★ Numerous success stories of relief being obtained, etc.

A MUST HAVE COLLECTION FOR ANY PRO SE USER!!!

★ COMING SOON ★
- The Pro Se Guide to Parole
- "DNA": Proving Your Innocence

We accept all forms of payment!

PayPal
VISA MasterCard DISCOVER BANK
venmo @FreebirdPublishers
Cash App $FreebirdPublishers

For more info on each book, order our catalog!
CATALOG ONLY $5 - SHIPS BY FIRST CLASS MAIL
We have created four different versions of our new catalog A: Complete B:No Pen Pal Content C:No Sexy Photo Content D:No Pen Pal and Sexy Content. Available in full Color or B&W (please specify) please make sure you order the correct catalog based on your prison mail room regulations. We are not responsible for rejected or lost in the mail catalogs. Send SASE for payment by stamp options.
ADDITIONAL OPTION: add $5 for Shipping with Tracking

<u>NO ORDER FORM NEEDED</u> CLEARLY WRITE ON PAPER & SEND PAYMENT TO:
FREEBIRD PUBLSIHERS 221 Pearl St., Ste. 541, North Dighton, MA 02764
www.Freebird Publishers.com Diane@FreebirdPublishers.com Text/Phone: 774-406-8682

PENPAL
Sites for Anyone

PENPAL SITES *for Anyone*

The following is a list of sites some pay, some free which will assist you in finding a pen pal. These sites aren't neccessarily prisoner friendly. You will have to have help from someone on the outside to list you and in some cases to monitor your profile.

aPenpals
www.apenpals.com
This site is great in the fact that you can sign up and select that you're looking for snail mail pen pals only. They even let you post your address on your profile. Once you're a member you can search for pen pals using their online search filter or just sit back and wait in hopes of one finding you.
Pricing: Free

International Pen Friends
www.ipfworld.com
If you are willing to pay for your pen pal, this site is highly recommended. They were established in 1967 and since then have processed over 2 million pen pal applications. This site asks you really detailed questions about your interests and the top countries you are interested in so they can match you up with the best pen pal for you. This is definitely one of the best sites to find snail mail pen pals.
Pricing: IPF bases their price on your age. Applicants from 15-20 years of age is $30, 21-60 years of age is $35, and applicants over 60 years of age is $30. The site does not accept checks or money orders. Whomever is paying must pay by paypal (no paypal account actually required, must at least have a credit card).

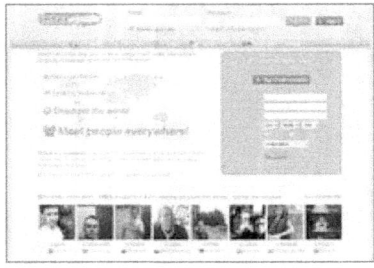

InterPals Penpals
www.interpals.net
InterPals is great for forging relationships with people around the world! You must sign up for a membership and complete your profile to be listed. Once listed you may connect with others and swap snail mail addresses. Most members on this site do not list their addresses online and some only wish to converse via e-mail and messaging.
Pricing: Free

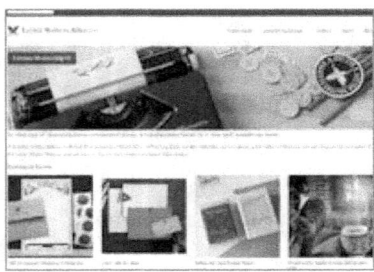

Letter Writers Alliance
www.letterwriters.org
Letter Writers Alliance requires a paid membership, but don't let that turn you away! If you're serious about letter writing and love having multiple pen pals, this site is the one for you! The website is dedicated to keeping the art of letter writing alive by linking you to other letter-enthusiasts and Letter Writers Alliance members. Ouside source required to manage site.
Pricing: $5 Lifetime Membership

PENPAL SITES *for Anyone*

Maarten's Snail Mail Pen Pals Online
maarten.daams.tripod.com
Maarten's has been online since 1998 and always has a new selection of pen pals to choose from. Like other free sites, you can choose to have your information listed or browse through the public listings. This site makes it easy to search by country, age, gender, and language. Most list only their e-mail address for first contact, but some list full mailing address. *Note some pen pals specifically list they do not wish to have correspondence with Inmates. Please obey these wishes so you are not banned from the site.
Pricing: Free

Pen Pal Hub
www.penpalhub.com
PenPalHub is a free platform to meet pen pals all over the world. Sign up for a free account, post your profile complete with your mailing address, browse other pen pals and use the online messaging to make your first contact.
Pricing: Free

Pen Pal World
www.penpalworld.com
Pen Pal World is a free site that allows you to directly contact other people seeking pen pals. All of the initial interaction happens through their site so none of your personal information is publicly displayed. Once you connect with a good match, you can choose to swap more information and begin writing letters. The downfall in this site is it will require more attention by your outside source. Your profile will be listed with NO address showing. Once you make contact with someone you're interested in (or they you) you will then swap address information and continue your friendship via snail mail.
Pricing: Free

Pen Pals Now
www.penpalsnow.com
Pen Pals Now is a free site. This site allows you to post your information so that others can find you. You can list a description, what you are looking for in a pen pal, etc. as well as your full snail mail address. You can also search for listings as well, although most people do not list their snail mail address, only an email address for first contact.
Pricing: Free

PENPAL SITES for Anyone

Pen Pal Party
penpalparty.com
This site is for pen paling only and has strict rules about it. If you're caught attempting to do anything other than find a pen pal you will be banned. Also they have specific rules for inmates. All is free but you have to disclose you are incarcerated as your occupation and have to have an email address on this one site and they do not allow direct posting of your snail mail address. There are almost 7500 pen pals on file that speak English as their first language. There are also about 14,000 pen pals on file from 166 countries. You can upload 100 words and one photo.
Pricing: Free

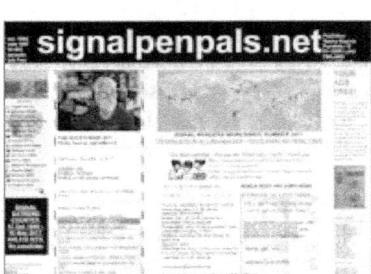

Sassociations
www.sassociations.net
Sassociations is a free pen pal site. It allows you to search for your pen pal by most recently added pen pals to age and gender. Some pen pals list their mailing addresses directly on their introduction, some only include an email address for first time contact. You can post your ad for free via their website.
Pricing: Free

Signals Pen Pals
signalpenpals.net
This list is published by Raimo Kaarna. There are over 50,000 pen pals on the site from all over the world. You can upload 100 words and one photo. US $10 to place pen pal ad and US $20 pen pal ad with photo. Send international stamped SASE or 3 FCS for information package. Be patient, overseas mail takes time.
Mail: Raimo Kaarna-XUA21
Purokatu 18
FI-15200 Lahti, Finland
Pricing: US $10, $20 Ad with Photo

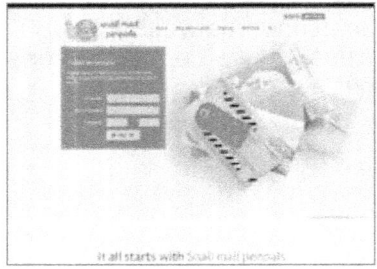

Snail Mail Pen Pals
www.snailmailpenpals.net
Sign up for free, fill out your profile and search the database of other users. Send online messages to exchange addresses.
Pricing: Free

PENPAL
Specialized Sites

PENPAL *Specialized Sites*

The following is a list of sites some pay, some free which will assist you in finding a pen pal. These sites aren't neccessarily prisoner friendly. You will have to have help from someone on the outside to list you and in some cases to monitor your profile.

CHRISTIAN PALS

Christian Cafe
www.ChristianCafe.com
Connecting Christian singles since 1999. More than just a dating site. Many of the members seek fellowship, support, advice and laughs through group conversation. Most popular are their Chrisitan Forums.
Pricing: Communicate for free.

Christian Crush
www.ChristianCrush.com
Christian Crush is an online dating site for Christians. If you're looking to meet someone and form an ongoing relationship with them that could possibly lead to something more Christain Crush could be for you. Christian Crush requires you to submit a profile with specific answers to questions like "What is your favorite Bible verse". You'll have to have someone on the outside to setup and maintain this site for you. Like other online dating sites you'll have to send messages online before being able to do so through snail mail.
Pricing: On ChristianCrush, it's always free to search profiles, see who's viewed you, send smiles, and send messages. However, you must be a subscribed member to include contact information in sent messages and to view received messages. $19.99 for full membership capabilities.

Christian Cupid
www.ChristianCupid.com
Are you looking for an online friendship that is romance free? Or do you want a safe approach to meeting your special single? If this is you then maybe you need to find a pen pal
Christian Cupid has a large database of Christians looking to find other christians.
Pricing: Free to review matches, paid for advanced messaging features.

Christian Mingle
www.ChristianMingle.com
Christian Mingle is a site that brings Christian singles together. If you're looking for a special someone who shares your same faith Christian Mingle may be the right choice for you. However this is a typical dating site in the fact that you will have to have someone do your corresponding via the internet. In most cases members will not give out their mailing addresses for a while.
Pricing: You may join for FREE, however in order to use most of the needed features you'll pay anywhere from $13.99/month to $29.99/month depending on the plan chosen.

PENPAL *Specialized Sites*

Christian Pen Pal Ministry
www.cppministry.com
Christian Pen Pal Ministry is a non profit org which strives to help lonely men and women who have accepted Jesus in finding a caring friend. Submit your information on their site or print a form online.
Mail: Pen Pal Connection
P.O. Box 11296
Hickory, NC 28603
Pricing: Please send donations or stamps if able.

INTERNATIONAL PALS

Global Pen Friends
www.globalpenfriends.com
Global Pen Friends has a Snailmail only section. You pay according to the number of address you wish to have. The site requires an email address and you'll have to have your outside person log in to search for penpals and purchase their addresses.
Pricing: 5 Snailmail addresses cost $10, 10 Snailmail Addresses costs $20.

Inter Pals Penpals
www.interpals.net
For over a decade, InterPals has been the Internet's premier free site for online correspondence, cultural exchange, and learning foreign languages. You will need outside help to create and manage your account. You can post your photo, a description and as much or as little infomation you wish. You must create an account to take advantage of all they have to offer, but it's free. Search for a friend by country, age, etc.
Pricing: Free

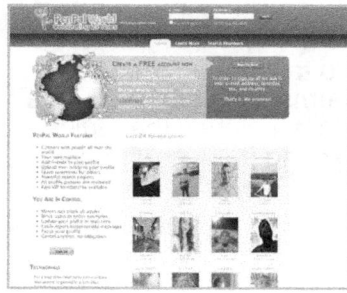

PenPal World
www.penpalworld.com
For over 25 years Pen Pal World has been connecting pen pals globally. It's a site where you can connect with over 3,000,000 pen pals from every country on the planet. The site allows you to contact and reply to up to three members within 24 hours. They do show your age, gener, and country as a point of interest. You can message them through their site without revealing an e-mail address. You can upload 100 words and one photo.
Pricing: Free

PENPAL *Specialized Sites*

LGBT PALS

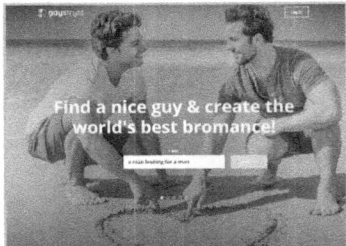

Gay Tryst
www.gaytryst.com
A dating site for men looking for fun and casual hookups with other men. Unlike other dating sites, this one doesn't include women at all - its for gay guys only. The majority of users are from the U.S. You can send up to three messages per day without paying.
Pricing: 3 Messages per day for Free, Pay for more services

Grindr
www.grindr.com
Available for gay, bi, trans, and other queer singles. Grindr is one of the best sites for gay men with a reputation of men seeking hookups with other men.
Pricing: $19.99/month or unlimited for $39.99/month

Pink Cupid
www.pinkcupid.com
PinkCupid is a leading lesbian dating site, helping thousands of lesbian singles find their match. As a large online lesbian community, they are one of the most trusted places for women to connect, fall in love, and get to know each other.
Pricing: Review Matches for free. Access to advance messaging features at paid prices

ONLINE DATING

eHarmony
eHarmony.com
The personality assessment and "something to talk about" feature gives the user pleanty of room to talk about themselves and their ideal partners. A more structured portion of the system includes the Guided Communication, a four step process for completing an overal profile.
Pricing: $26.95/month

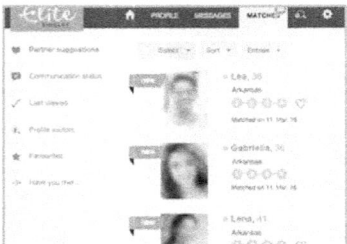

Elite Singles
elitesingles.com
With more than 67% of its members holding either a bachelor's, masters, or doctorate degree, EliteSingles.com has established itself as the premier dating site for educated proffessionals looking for long term partners. It also has a unique questionare to ensure high quality compatability results.
Pricing: Starting at $31.95/month

Match
match.com
Experts say that Match.com has led to more dates, marriages and relationships than any other site. Its impressive user base and success rate make it top of the list in overall ranking.
Pricing: Free

OkCupid
okcupid.com
OkCupid is slightly different than you're normal online dating site. It actually asks you a series of interesting questions to get to know who you are on a deeper level. Then it's super-smart algorithm then uses your answers to discover people that you'll like. You can then connect with them via online messaging.
Pricing: Free

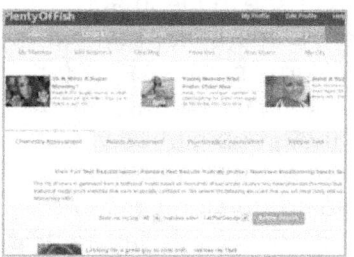
Pleanty of Fish
http://pof.com
Pleanty of Fish, also known as POF is one of the more popular dating sites for singles. It offers a free membership and free messaging system. The basic search on POF is far more complex than most giving you a better means of thinning down the crowd of potentially good matches.
Pricing: Free Membership and Premium for $5.95-9.80/month

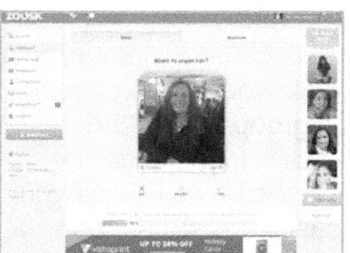
Zoosk
zoosk.com
Zoosk is a fast-growing site that offers a unique dating experience for its users. Zoosk has become one of the largest online dating sites thanks to its integration with social networks and smartphones. It's a popular choice for daters looking for casual dates or even deep relationships, and its more than 35 million users can view and communicate with potential dates via the Internet, iPhones and social networking services like Facebook.
Pricing: Starting at $12.49/month

KEEP IN MIND...

Online Dating websites aren't meant for prisoners, unfortunately. If you choose to have someone create a profile for you be sure that they will check it regularly and report back to you. And as always, honesty is the best policy. Let your online connections know that you're serving time. They may surprise you.

My loved one in prison had me set him up on pleantyoffish.com a good while back. It was hard to keep the attention once we told them that he was incarcerated, but he did gain a couple of connections that became his pen pal so it's not unheard of.

PENPAL Social Media

Never underestimate the power of social media when it comes to finding a great penpal. Unfortunately you'll need someone to help you with this project, but it can prove to be very rewarding.

If don't have a facebook account, you'll need to have someone set you up with one before doing the following, but it's fairly simple and within a few minutes you'll be ready to go.

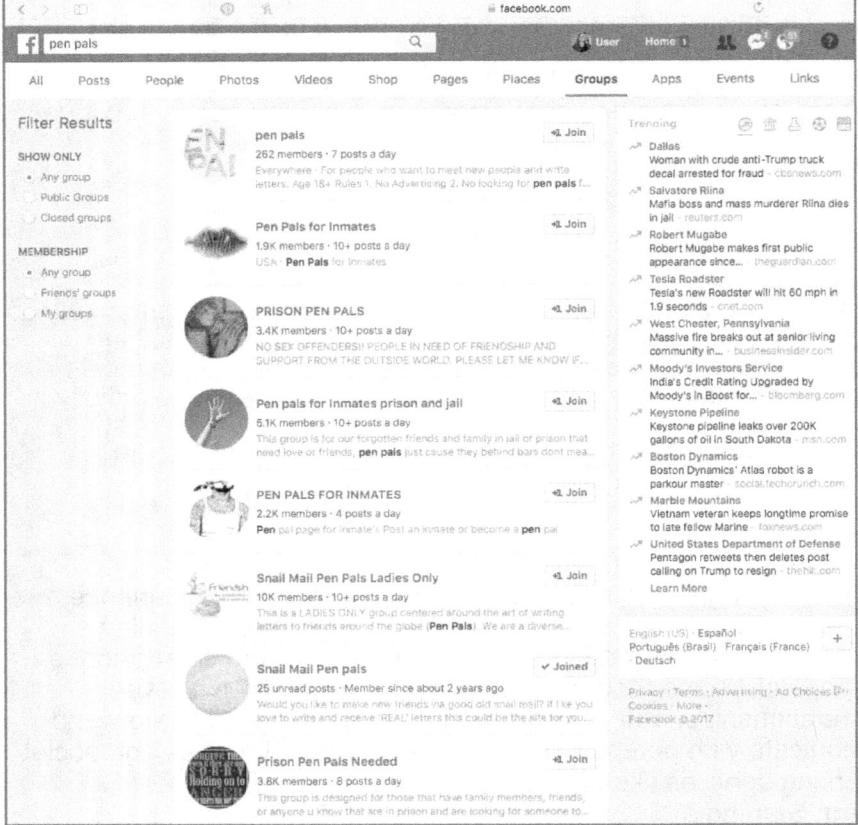

Once logged in you can type into the search bar at the top "pen pals." Following that click on the button at the top that says "groups" this will filter your results for ONLY groups for pen pals.

As you can see in the image to the left, a search for pen pal groups returns many results (of course not all are shown). Below each of the group names you'll see the amount of members within the group along with the amount of posts each day as well as a brief description.

In order to become a member of these groups you'll have to "join". Facebook groups are FREE. Once you click join, the group administrator has to approve you. In most cases this will happen within 24 hours.

Before posting anything to these group pages make sure you read their rules. Some don't allow you to post your address, just an introduction with a "message me if you'd like to swap info" kind of thing. Most don't allow fowl language and if you violate their rules they have the right to remove you from the group. They also do not allow spaming and will not tolerate you posting your information multiple times a day. I suggest joining multiple pen pal groups and posting your infomration to each. If you're not getting reponses repost to the site. Most will allow you to repost weekly.

When posting you'll want to include your name, age, sex, a brief description about yourself and what you're looking for in a pen pal and possibly a picture. Postings with pictures definitely attract more of a response. It would be ideal to post your address and include the fact that you're only looking for snail mail pen pal and not email or facebook pals. Again, check the rules before posting your address as some groups do not allow it.

To the right you'll see an example of a posting on Snail Mail Pen Pals group within Facebook. You'll notice the user who posted the request did not list an address. On this group they suggest you PM (personal message) your prosepective pen pal with that information.

Many of the prisoner related pen pal groups do allow posting your address though and I'd definitely suggest putting your information on as many of those as possible. The more your name is out there the more possibilities you have of finding that pen pal that makes it all worthwhile.

Rember to keep in mind the same tips as previously mentioned when writing your "profile" for these pages. Being honest, positive, and saying what you're looking for in a pen pal will definitely yield the best results.

A quick search for Pen Pal Groups on Facebook returned the following (which is only a partial listing):

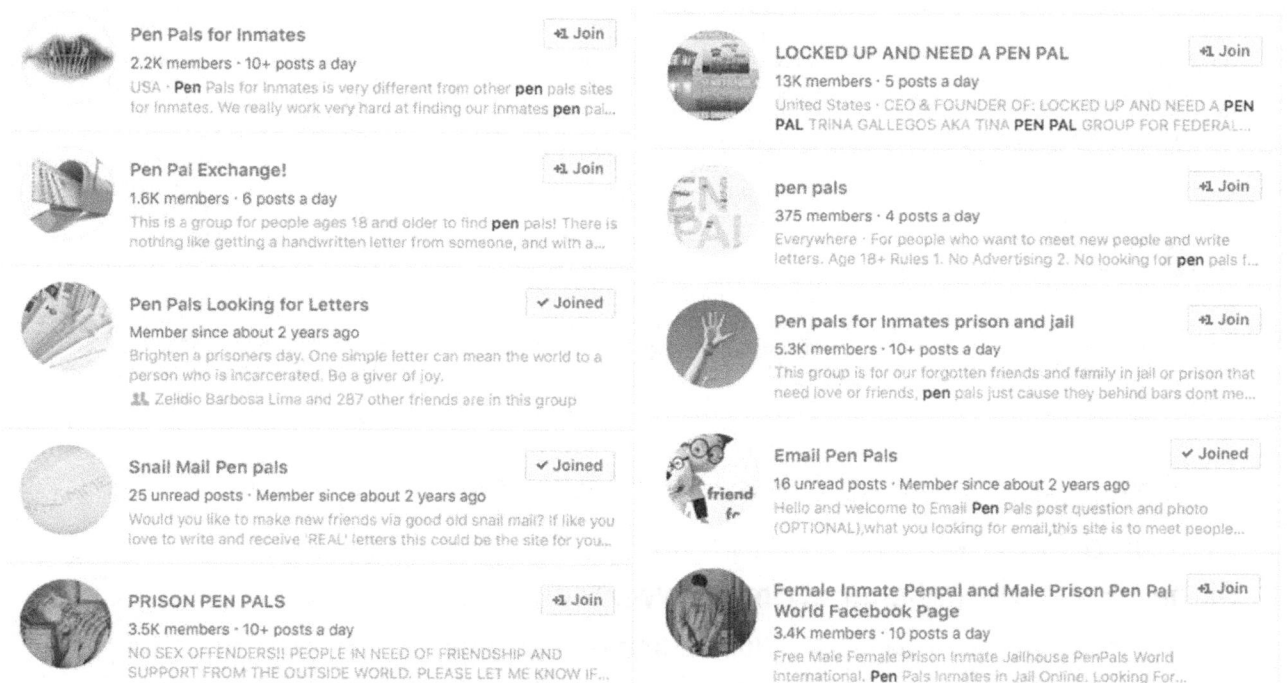

Pen Pals: A Personal Guide for Prisoners

FREEBIRD PUBLISHERS
REFERENCE BOOKS

Only $34.99
includes S/H with Tracking
SOFTCOVER, 8" x 10", 360 pages

Only $31.99
includes S/H with Tracking
SOFTCOVER, 8" x 10", 240+ pages

Only $30.99 for both
includes S/H with Tracking
SOFTCOVER, 8" x 10", 210+ pages

Things don't magically change after you get kicked out of prison. Life starts all over again but there's a catch, having a record impacts almost every part of your life. With this book you'll find out how to prepare for life as an ex-offender. Filled with insights, advice, contacts, and exercises the information strikes legal, personal and professional levels. A real world guide for minimizing disruptions and maximizing success. Life With A Record helps make sense of the major challenges facing ex-offenders today. Ten hard hitting chapters outline the purpose of makinga Strategic Reentry Plan and making peace with supervisors, family, your community and your future.
Inside you will find: How to rebuild your credit, halfway house rules and terms, special grants and loans to finance education, job training or start a business, legal tips for dealing with discrimination, hundreds of reentry contacts and so much more!

Don't let a prison cell keep you from interacting with the world. Jailhouse publishing is possible! In fact, our new book gives authors the blueprint for first time to full time success.
In 30 information-dense chapters you'll DISCOVER how to turn your way with words into wads of cash.
• How to brainstorm, outline and then write your book.
• What to negotiate for in publishing agreements and other binding documents!
• Learn to write one book but sell it in multiple formats.
• Effectively make yourself irresisstable to editors–who'll stay on your team for years.
• What to do once you get published so your readers keep coming back.
• Learn self-publishing tools on Amazon, iTunes, Scrivener and beyond.
• Find useful creative writing advice
• How to design a press kit that empowers your publicity campaign
• And more!

First adopted in 1975, the Federal Rules of Evidence codify the evidence law that applies in United States federal courts. In addition, many states in the United States have either adopted the Federal Rules of Evidence, with or without local variations, or have revised their own evidence rules or codes to at least partially follow the federal rules.
In general, the purpose of rules of evidence is to regulate the evidence that the jury may use to reach a verdict.
The Federal Rules of Criminal Procedure govern how federal criminal prosecutions are conducted in United States district courts and the general trial courts of the U.S. government. The admissibility and use of evidence in crimi- nal proceedings (as well as civil) is governed by the separate Federal Rules of Evidence.
The rules are promulgated by the Supreme Court of the United States, pursuant to its statu- tory authority.

No Order Form Needed: Clearly write on paper & send with payment to:

Freebird Publishers 221 Pearl St., Ste. 541, North Dighton, MA 02764
Diane@FreebirdPublishers.com   www.Freebirdpublishers.com
We accept all forms of payment. Plus Venmo & CashApp!
Venmo: @FreebirdPublishers   CashApp: $FreebirdPublishers

FREEBIRD PUBLISHERS
SELF-HELP

Only $20.99
Includes S/H with Tracking
SOFTCOVER, 6" x 9", 70+ pages

Greatness lies within many of my brothers and sisters. The problem is we tend to find ourselves incarcerated before we discover this greatness. Our thought patterns and consistent inability to think on a positive level leads us straight to prison. Thinking is very critical to one's success, failure, and survival. Every decision requires thinking. If not, many actions will be done on impulse. And impulsive behavior tends to bring about situations from which one needs to be rescued. If the impulses aren't tamed or controlled, the behavior patterns will be present in each stage of life. Maybe this is the reason I see so many 40-year-olds that lack self-control or the ability to deal with some of life's simplest problems. They can't attack the situations from a professional, calm, and diplomatic standpoint. S.T.O.P. was written as a movement to help promote a greater thinking process - a thinking process I believe will slow down the recidivism rate within our communities.

Only $20.99
Includes S/H with Tracking
SOFTCOVER, 8" x 10", 240+ pages

In life, true strength comes from never letting an experience define you. There is always a reason for everything - steppingstones on a path to better destinations. Our words have immense creative power and determine where our paths will lead us. If we put positive words into the world we create reality from with them."Positive, creative and powerful," is how the Bible says we were created, and it explains the capabilities we all possess from birth. We are gods - creators. We create our destiny with our words ... good or bad ... and we are responsible. Of course, that means that we are always capable of changing the course of our lives, by speaking good words.This book will literally change your life and hopefully open your eyes to your own creative power.A must-read for everyone!
A man's future consists of the faith inside of him. Whatever that faith is, so shall it become his reality.-The Bhagavagita

Only $20.99
Includes S/H with Tracking
SOFTCOVER, 6" x 9", 100+ pages

Parent to Parent: Raising Children from Prison entails the painful and real emotions a parent experiences while incarcerated and separated from their children. The book explains how an incarcerated parent must discover, find, and explore himself before he can be beneficial to his children. It involves the personal sharing of the author's story, and how he used many resources including, but not limited to, self-reflection and self-examination in order to overcome the many past hurts he experienced. He discusses the importance of maintaining mental and physical health, how to achieve it, and in other chapters, he discusses the difference between discipline and punishment, the importance of communication, and healing, forgiveness, and love. Also, the author offers more in-depth discussions as well as techniques and ideas of how parents can be actively involved with their children while incarcerated. Once a parent begins to make changes in his/her own life, then they can begin to make a positive influence in their children's lives.

No Order Form Needed: Clearly write on paper & send with payment to:

Freebird Publishers 221 Pearl St., Ste. 541, North Dighton, MA 02764
Diane@FreebirdPublishers.com   www.Freebirdpublishers.com
We accept all forms of payment. Plus Venmo & CashApp!
Venmo: @FreebirdPublishers   CashApp: $FreebirdPublishers

PENPAL
Mail Art & Ideas

PENPAL
Mail Art & Ideas

Mail is always much more fun when you get creative with it. Not only can it be fun for you, but for your pen pal. Think about how much more interesting it would be to pull out a booklet written letter, a letter with doodles or creative embellishments, or even to see a fancy envelope arrive from your pen pal (if your facility allows). If you put more time and effort into your pen pals they will be even more impressed. Feel free to use these ideas, trace some fonts onto your letters, or just simply use this section as a guide to your creativity with your pen pal letters.

MAKE A MINI BOOKLET

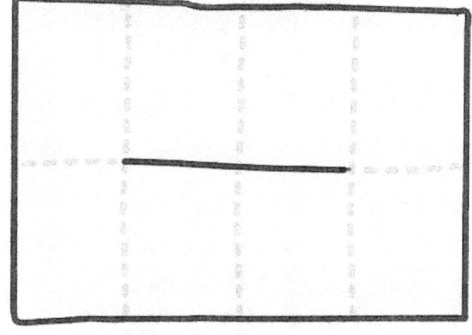

Step 1
GET A PIECE OF PAPER (8.5 x 11")
FOLD
CUT

Step 2
FOLD FOLLOWING THE LONG SIDE.

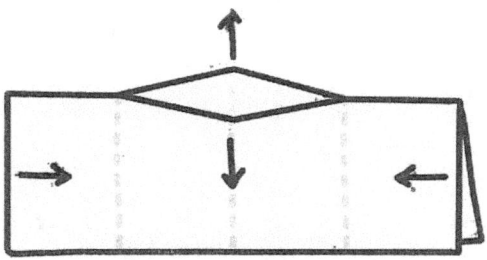

Step 3
PULL ON THE POINTS OUTWARDS FROM THE HOLE AND PUSH THE ENDS INWARDS TO THE CENTER

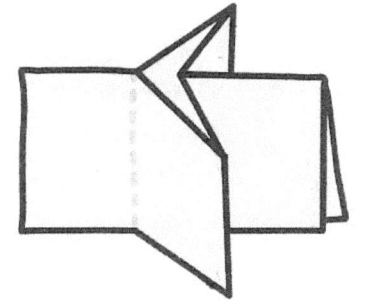

Step 4
CONTINUE UNTIL YOU GET A SORT OF PLUS-SHAPE.

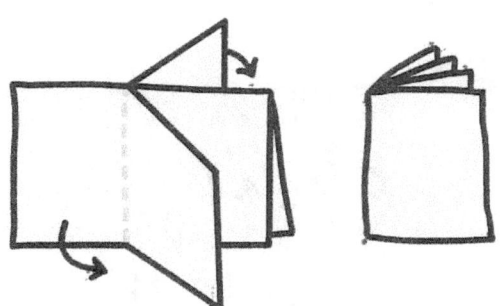

Step 5
NOW FOLD THE TWO OUTER FLAPS OVER THE OTHERS AND TADAA! A BOOKLET. WRITE A LETTER AND / OR DECORATE IT.

ENVELOPE Art & Ideas

CREATIVE ENVELOPE ADDRESSING

You know the standard (boring) way to address an envelope. Yes, it may be the correct way but if your facility will allow, here are some ideas on how to make it look a bit more appealing. We are all guilty of "judging a book by it's cover" with these envelopes your mail immediately looks more interesting.

Note: The names and addresses below are fictional.

miss **CYNTHIA PARKER**
1009 Cedar Point Ln.
Austin • Texas
12345

JANE
D • O • E
123 Address
DAMARISCOTTA
MAINE • 01234

Krista Smith
123 ADDRESS
HOUSTON, TX 77777

kelli harper
1212 Ocean Drive
Santa Barbara, CA
•••••••••••• 54321 ♥

Shelly Williams
2222 James Ave.
Milwaukee, WI 12345

PLEASE DELIVER TO **SARAH**
Miller
123 Hartford Dr.
Elk River, MN 54321

ENVELOPE LINING

Lining envelopes is an easy, instant upgrade to your letters, and even if you claim you're not crafty, you will be able to do this. You can use almost any paper imaginable to make envelope liners – solids, patterns, fine paper, newspaper, magazine pages, crossword puzzles, even photocopies of pictures. All you need is the paper you're going to use as lining, an envelope, a pair of scissors and some glue.

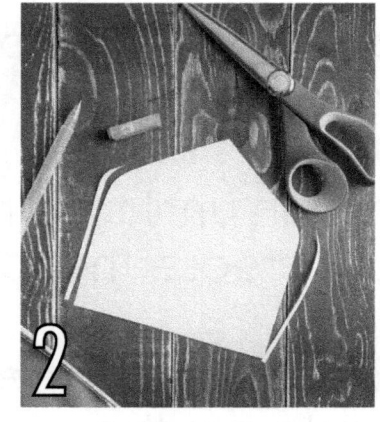

1. Create your lining template by tracing one envelope onto a blank page.
2. Cut out the template, then trim it about 1/4 of an inch smaller all the way around.
3. Use your template to trace the area of the page lining of your choice and cut it out.
4. Slide lining into envelope, being sure that it is lined up below the adhesive on the envelope flap.
5. Fold lining down (like the flap) and glue the back side of the lining. Allow to dry before inserting your letter.

ENVELOPE *Art & Ideas*

HOW TO TURN YOUR LETTER INTO AN ENVELOPE

You know the standard (boring) way to address an envelope. Yes, it may be the correct way but if your facility will allow, here are some ideas on how to make it look a bit more appealing. We are all guilty of "judging a book by it's cover" with these envelopes your mail immediately looks more interesting.

1. Start with a letter on 8.5" x 11" paper turned in landscape orientation

2. Fold both top corners in until they meet in the middle and carefully crease the folds.

3. Fold the bottom edge of the paper up until it meets the bottom edge of the triangles.

4. Fold in both sides towards the center, lining them up along the center fold.

5. Fold Down the top triangle, aligning it with the other edges.

6. Secure with glue or tape.

Letter writing is the only device for combining solitude with good company. —lord byron

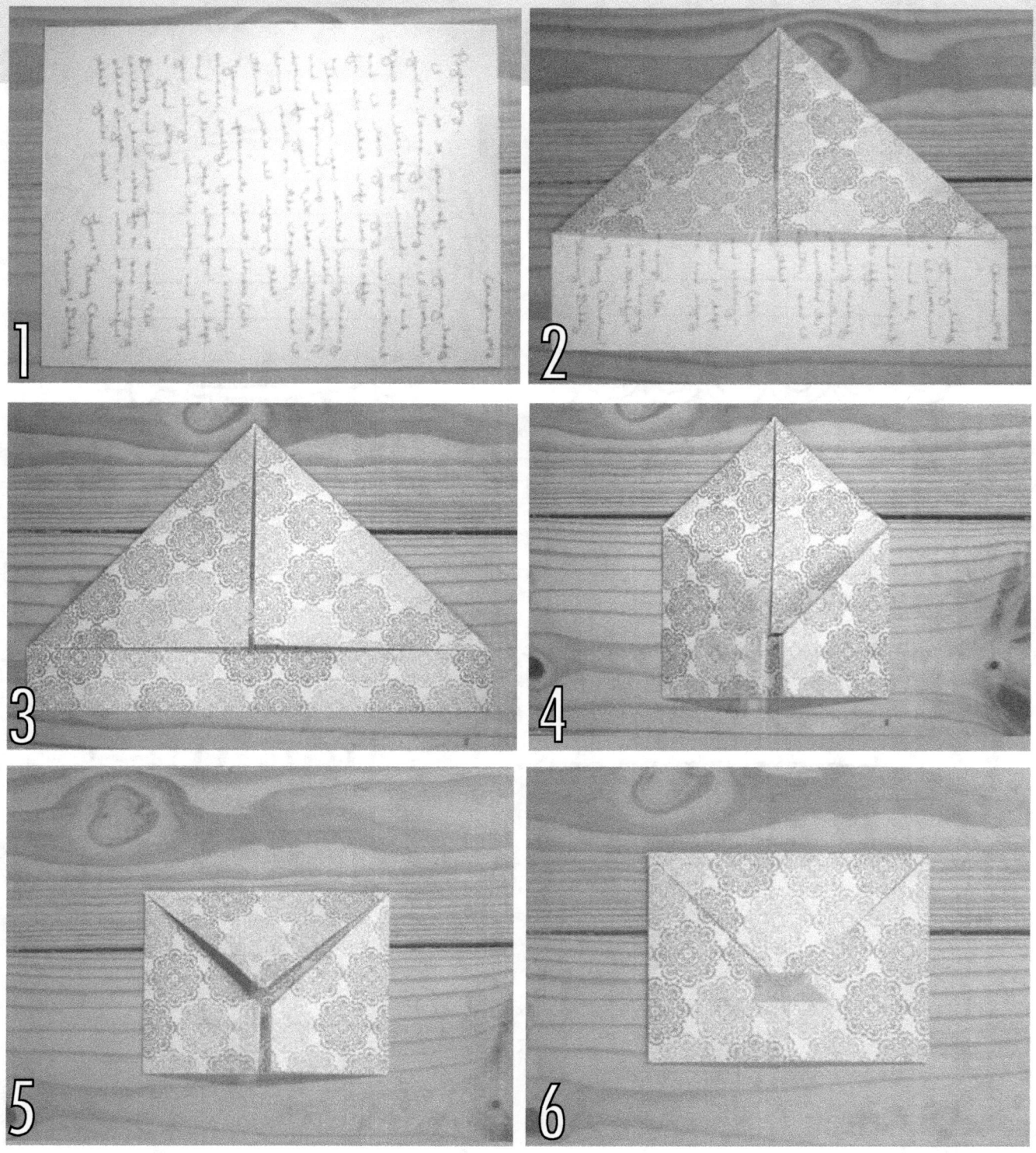

Pen Pals: A Personal Guide for Prisoners

ENVELOPE Art & Ideas

ADDRESS LABELS

Copy, draw them on your envelopes or cut these labels out and affix them to your envelopes (if your facility allows).

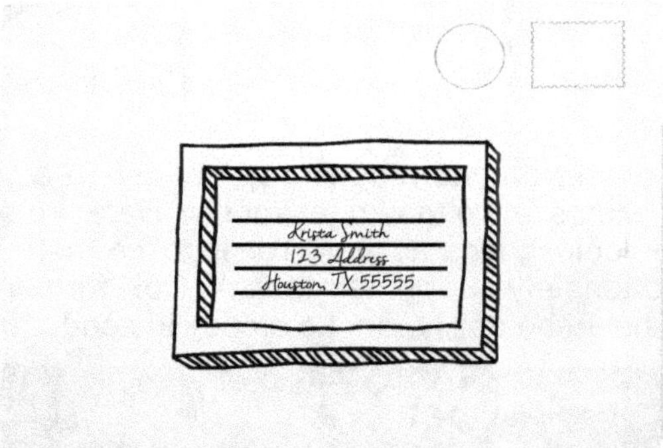
Krista Smith
123 Address
Houston, TX 55555

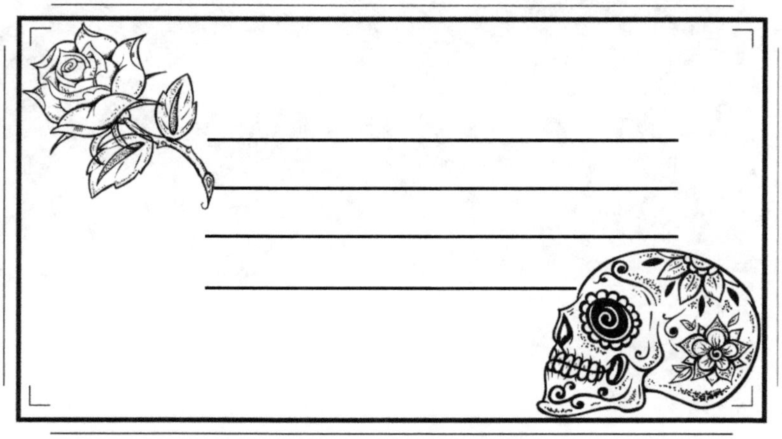

HOW TO Remove Book Pages Neatly

On occassion you may find something in a book that you want to share with your Pen Pal. Tearing it out can sometimes leave the edges messy. Here are a couple of methods to help you clean up those lines and keep your book looking nice as well. You'll notice there are pages of this book that are meant to be pulled out and used. Unfortunately our printer doesn't allow for perforated pages at this time, so hopefully this method will help. Or if you have the ability - make a copy instead.

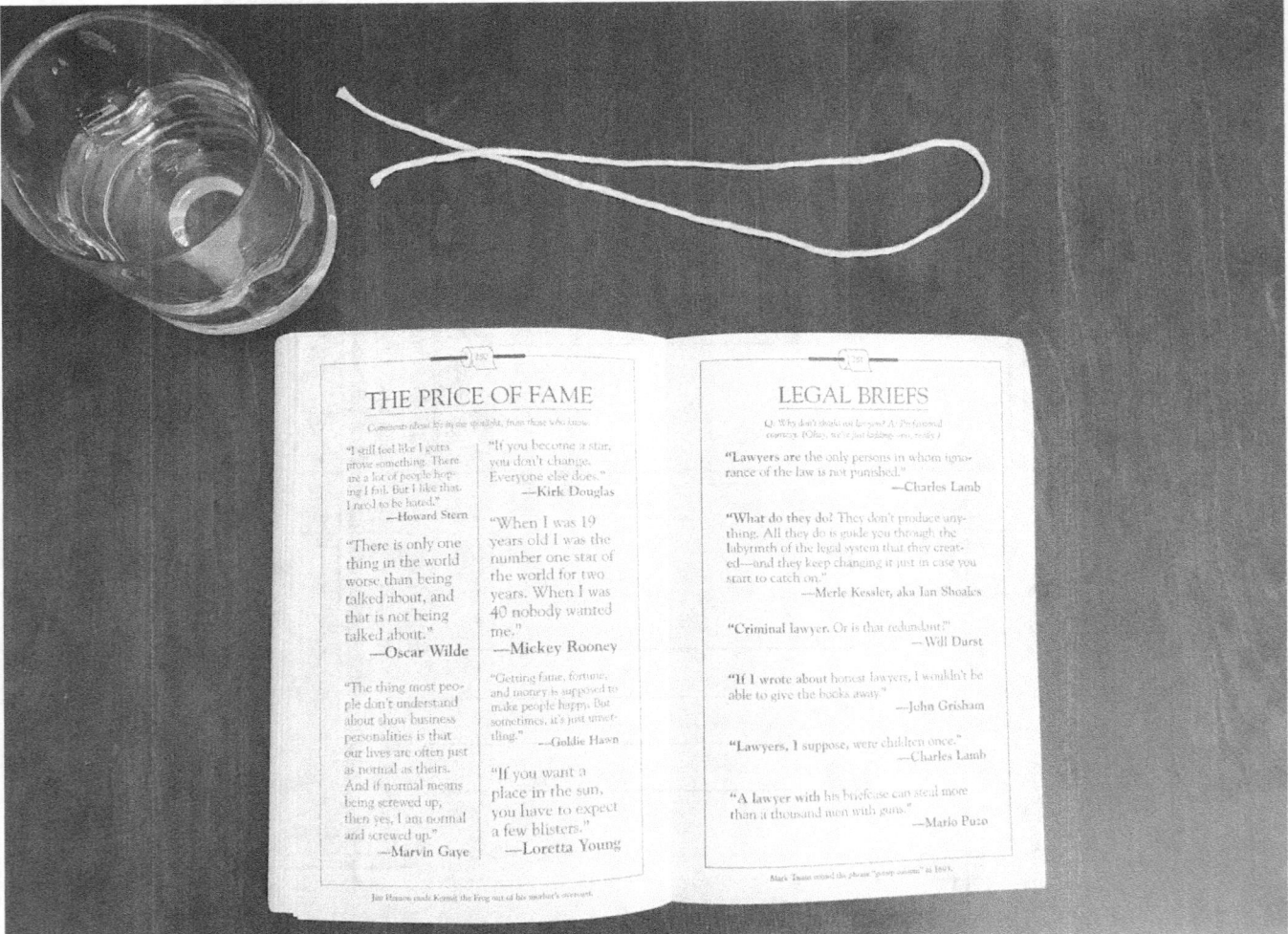

1 Gather Materials: You'll need a piece of string (just some plain ol' string, nothing fancy.), the book you want to take a page from, and water.

2 Cut a length of string longer than the book you want to remove the page from. It doesn't matter how long, just so long as it's longer than the book plus enough extra to be able to grasp it.

3 Soak the string in water.

4 Place the string on the page you want to cut out (or if there's 2 pages you want, put it between those two pages.

5 Pull it tight so it is straight on the page, and then pull it close to the binding of the book.

6 Close the book and hold it tightly closed for 10-30 seconds depending on how thick the pages are. With this book I reccommend 15 seconds. If you can see the wet line you're probably good.

7 Now open the book and examine the page - it should have a line where it's wet where the string was, and therefore very weak along this line.

8 Tear the page out carefully - it should tear cleanly on the line. If not, wet the string more and put it back on the already weak area and do it again.

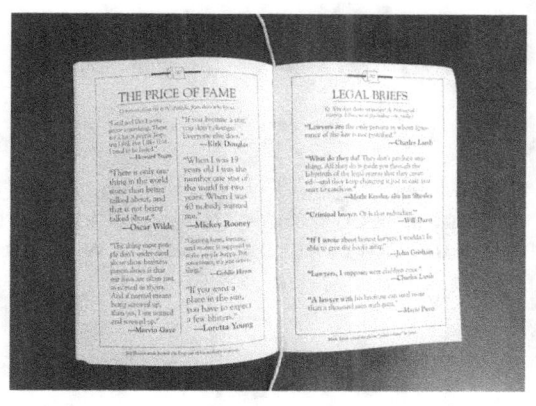

Tips: Depending on the type of string you use you may have to somewhat ring it out. I did. You want the string to be saturated but not dripping water. You don't want to mess up any other pages of your book. As with anything like this practice makes perfect. I tried this method myself several times. The first time it worked well however my line wasn't completely stright. It's important to put the string in and pull tight. Be sure to test this method out first on a page or book that you're not needing for your project.

BOOK PAGE ART

Want to impress your Pen Pal? You can use the pages of an old book as a canvas for a beautiful piece of art. Maybe you've read the same book alongside your pen pal? Perhaps pull a page from the book that means something to the both of you and paint a simple picture on top of it. Painting with watercolor on top of a book page can produce a beautiful result. The combination of opague words and translucent color is mesmerizing. Add in the details with a pen and your artwork pops. Here's a few examples that some artists on Etsy.com have achieved.

FONTS / *Lettering*

Want to use some fancy lettering but you're not an artist? Here are some fonts you can practice writing or even trace onto your pen pals letters. Use them to write their name at the top of the letter or on the envelope, use them to write a quote, etc.

Aa Bb Cc Dd
Ee Ff Gg Hh
Ii Jj Kk Ll Mm
Nn Oo Pp Qq
Rr Ss Tt Uu Vv
Ww Xx Yy Zz

Aa Bb Cc Dd Ee
Ff Gg Hh Ii Jj Kk
Ll Mm Nn Oo Pp
Qq Rr Ss Tt Uu
Vv Ww Xx Yy Zz

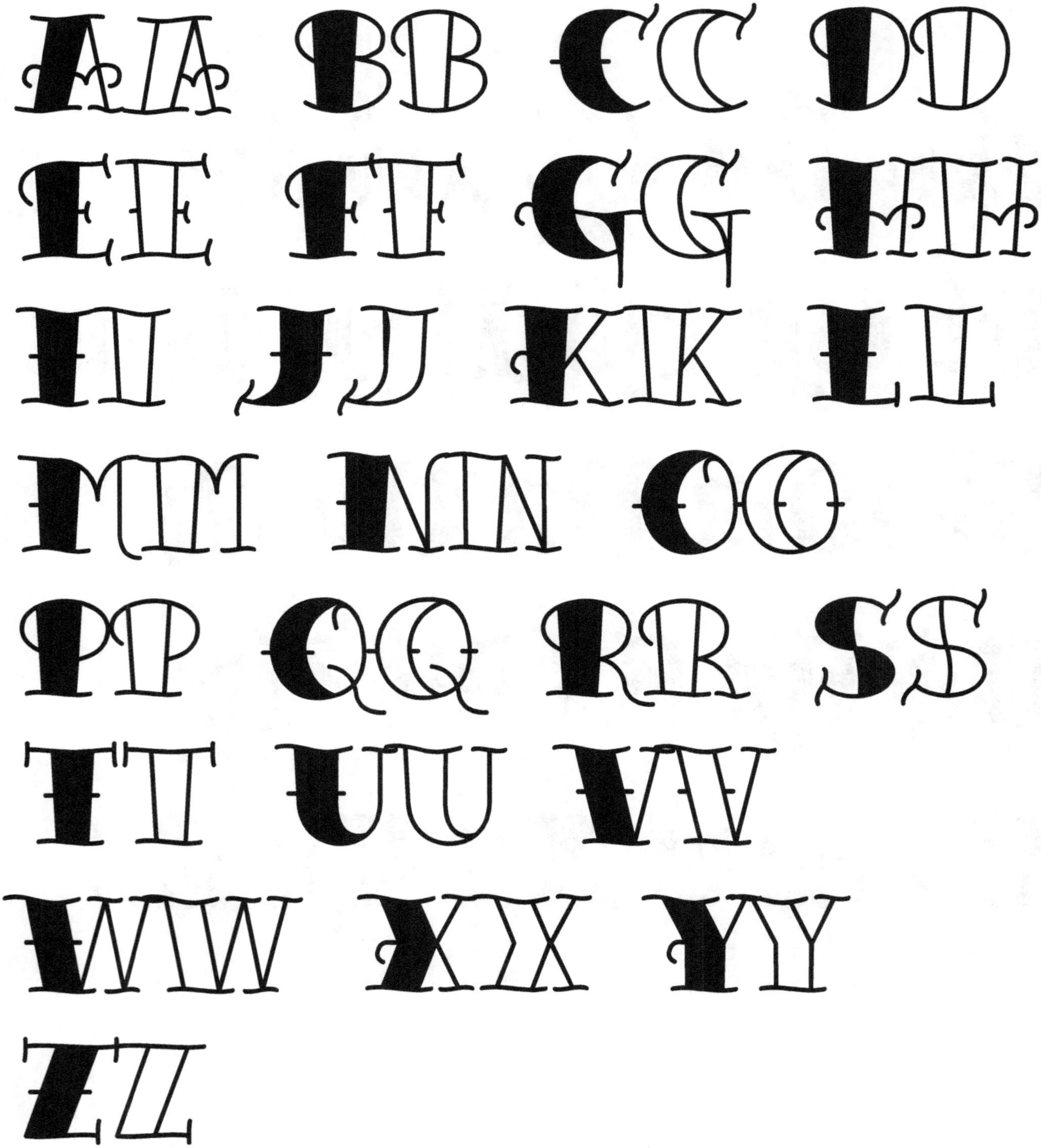

AA BB CC DD
EE FF GG HH
II JJ KK LL
MM NN OO
PP QQ RR SS
TT UU VV
WW XX YY
ZZ

Aa Bb Cc Dd
Ee Ff Gg Hh Ii
Jj Kk Ll Mm Nn
Oo Pp Qq Rr
Ss Tt Uu Vv Ww
Xx Yy Zz

Aa Bb Cc Dd
Ee Ff Gg Hh Ii
Jj Kk Ll Mm
Nn Oo Pp Qq
Rr Ss Tt Uu Vv
Ww Xx Yy Zz

A B C D E F G
H I J K L M N
O P Q R S T
U V W X Y Z

Aa Bb Cc Dd
Ee Ff Gg Hh Ii
Jj Kk Ll Mm
Nn Oo Pp Qq
Rr Ss Tt Uu Vv
Ww Xx Yy Zz

Aa Bb Cc Dd
Ee Ff Gg Hh Ii
Jj Kk Ll Mm
Nn Oo Pp Qq
Rr Ss Tt Uu Vv
Ww Xx Yy Zz

a B C D E
F G H I J
K L M N
O P Q R S
T U V W
X Y Z

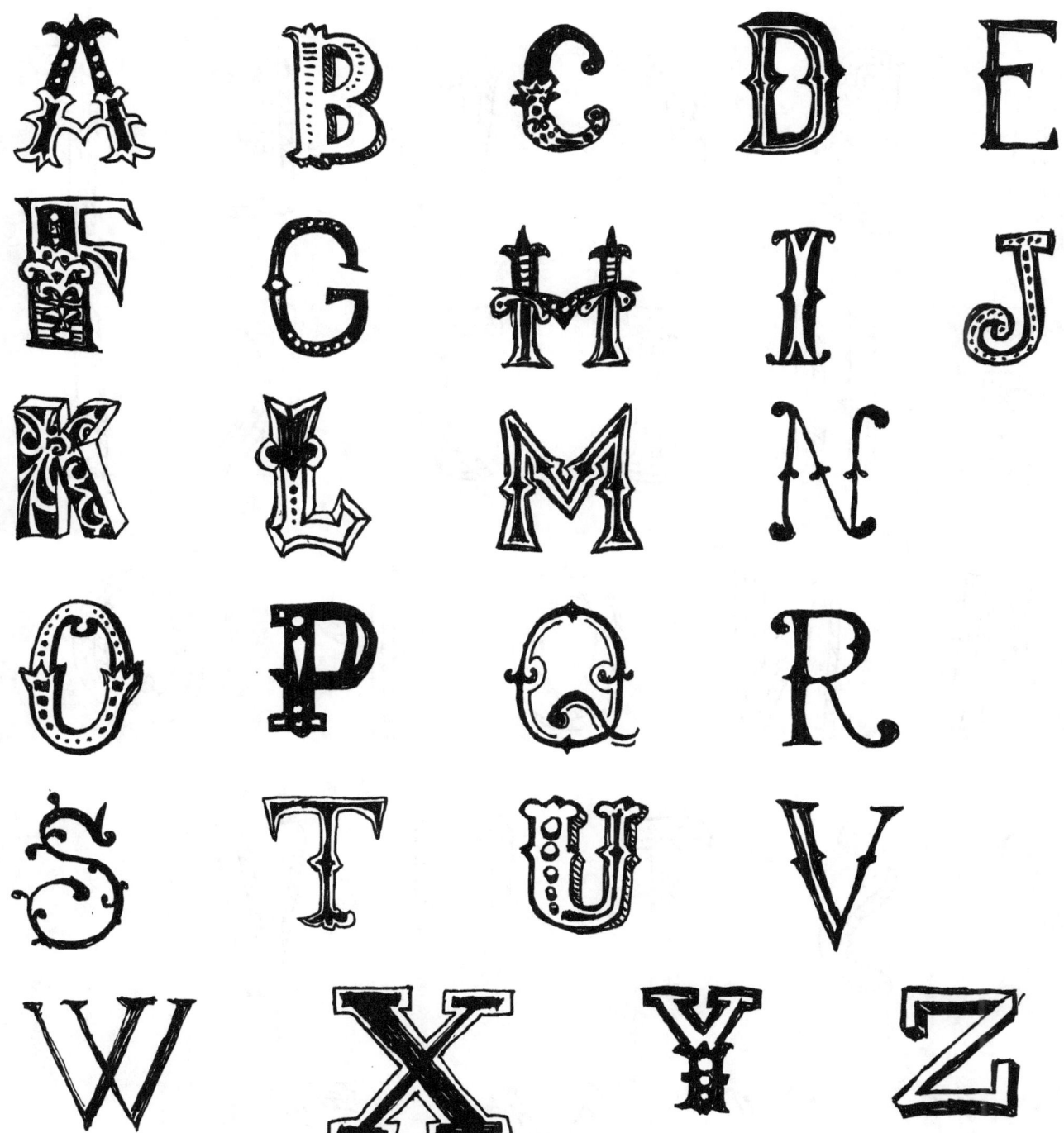

A B C D E
F G H I J
K L M N
O P Q R S
T U V W
X Y Z

Aa Bb Cc Dd
Ee Ff Gg Hh
Ii Jj Kk Ll
Mm Nn Oo Pp
Qq Rr Ss Tt
Uu Vv Ww Xx
Yy Zz

Interested in fonts and lettering?

The following books are available for purchase through Freebird Publishers. Send orders to: Freebird Publishers | 221 Pearl St, Ste. 541 | North Dighton, MA 02764. Price includes S/H.

 Creative Lettering: Techniques and Tips from Top Artists.

$29.99

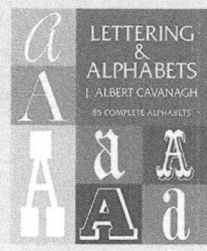 Lettering and Alphabets: 85 Complete Alphabets

$30.99

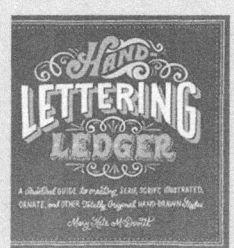 Hand Lettering Ledger

$42.99

Pen Pals: A Personal Guide for Prisoners

DOODLES & Embellishments

Doodles make a plain piece of paper fun! Trace some of these doodles or use them as inspiration to create your own. Even people who aren't artistic can create cool doodles! They can be simple shapes and lines or actual objects. Use them as borders, use them as space fillers or just use them anywhere. Color them in or leave them plain. Regardless, doodles definitely spice up a simple letter.

Doodle Frames

Doodle Borders

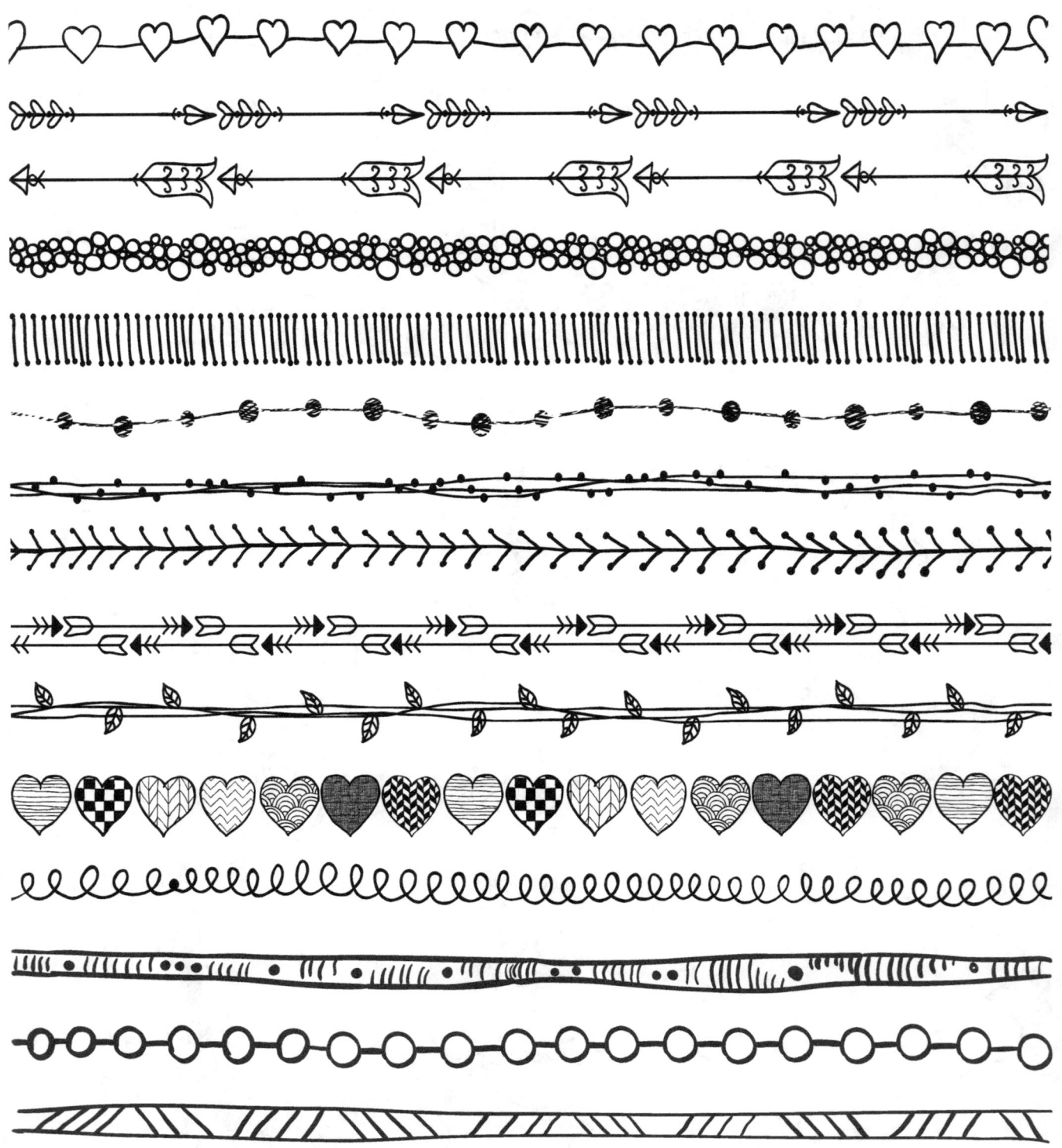

Doodle Faces

Pen Pals: A Personal Guide for Prisoners

Doodle Collage

Create a doodle collage on one idea or subject and base your doodle around it. Below "I Love You" with doodles resembling love all around. You can do this with any subject or even with no specific subject at all.

RANDOM DOODLE IDEAS

RANDOM DOODLE IDEAS

Interested in more doodle ideas?

The following books are available for purchase through Freebird Publishers. Send orders to Freebird Publishers | 221 Pearl St, Ste. 541 | North Dighton, MA 02764. Price includes S/H.

Creative Doodling and Beyond

$35.99

Doodle Art Handbook

$30.99

MAKE YOUR OWN *Greeting Cards*

You don't have to be an artist to make your own greeting cards. You can make cards as simple as folding a piece of paper and writing something clever on the front. Add a small doodle, a work of art, or nothing at all. Your pen pal will understand and appreciate the gesture. Here are some ideas to get you started.

Greeting card images reprinted from Etsy.com. Purchase handmade items at Etsy.com

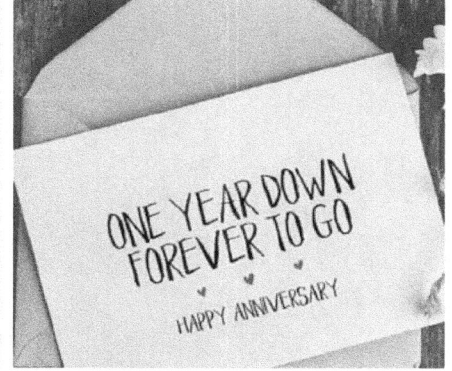

Pen Pals: A Personal Guide for Prisoners

MAKE YOUR OWN *Greeting Cards*

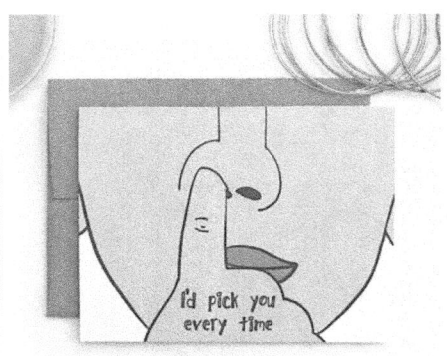

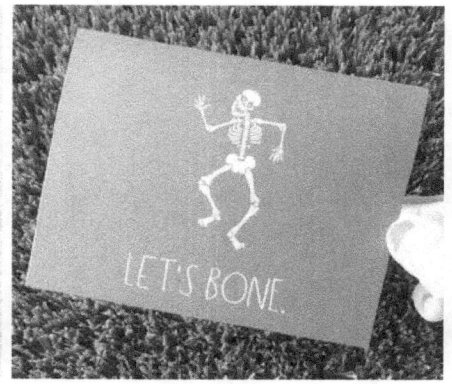

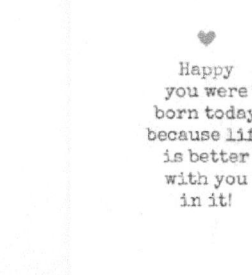
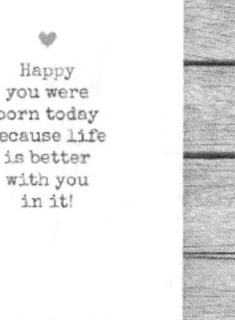

MAKE YOUR OWN *Greeting Cards*

our gifts are made in America!

FREEBIRD PUBLISHERS
GIFTS

Only $19.99
FREE S/H
SOFTCOVER, 8.5" x 11", 110+ pages

ALL IN ONE FULL COLOR BOOK!

- Baby
- Birthday
- Care Packages
- Children's Gifts
- Easter
- Fall Gifts
- Father's Day
- Gardening Gifts
- Get Well
- Gifts for Men
- Gifts for Women
- Gourmet
- Halloween
- Meat & Cheeses
- Mini Baskets
- Mother's Day
- New Home
- Pet Gifts
- Plush
- Snack Baskets
- Special Diets
- Specialty Foods
- Sports
- St. Patrick's
- Sympathy
- Thank You
- Valentine's
- Wedding & Romance
- And More!

Full size, color GIFT LOOK BOOK with hundreds of our high quality handcrafted gifts to choose from, all made in the U.S.A. We offer complete line of gift baskets that have been custom designed. We have flowers that get delivered fresh in bud-form so they open up to bloom in front of your loved ones. Our chocolates are of the finest quality, all made fresh. All of our gifts are skillfully featured in detailed full color photographs.

With every book receive a $19.99 Voucher from our GIFT LOOK BOOK for $95.00 or more. (not including shipping & handling. good towards a purchase of any gift order

---

TOUCHSTONE CRYSTAL BY SWAROVSKI
SWAROVSKI CRYSTAL ON THE RED CARPET

only $9.99

All our jewels feature fine quality SWAROVSKI Crystals and SWAROVSKI Zirconia, the finest simulated diamond in the world.

WANT TO SEE MORE OF OUR
SWAROVSKI CRYSTAL JEWELRY...

Order our full size, color catalog with hundreds of our high quality, beautifully handcrafted jewelry pieces to by Swarovski Collections that have been custom designed. Swarovski's rich heritage of craftsmanship, creativity and innovation ensures that the quality, cut and finish of every crystal is second to none. All of our jewelry is skillfully featured in detailed full color photographs on 8.5 X 11" 80 glossy pages with full descriptions & prices. Over 400 pieces of high quality jewelry and accent pieces.

How to order: on blank paper, write Touchstone Crystal Catalog, and include your complete contact info with payment of $9.99 to Freebird Publishers. All catalogs are mailed USPS tracking with packing slip/invoice.

With every catalog receive a $9.99 Voucher, good towards a purchase of Touchstone Crystal by Swarovski for $50.00 or more. (not including sales tax and S/H)

No Order Form Needed: Clearly write on paper & send with payment to:
Freebird Publishers 221 Pearl St., Ste. 541, North Dighton, MA 02764
Diane@FreebirdPublishers.com   www.Freebirdpublishers.com
We accept all forms of payment. Plus Venmo & CashApp!
Venmo: @FreebirdPublishers   CashApp: $FreebirdPublishers

PENPAL *Greeting Cards*

Not in the mood to create your own greeting card? Use one of our premade cards. Carefully tear/pull/cut out our cards. Leave them as is, or color them for a more personal touch.

Note: Pull out pages and fold along the straight line to create your greeting card. For help on how to cleanly remove the pull out pages of this book refer to page 74.

hello there

THOUGH MILES MAY SEPARATE US, MY LOVING THOUGHTS ARE WITH YOU.

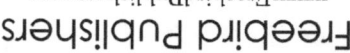

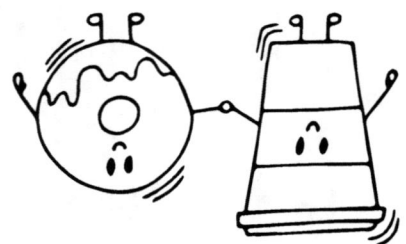

Freebird Publishers
www.FreebirdPublishers.com

I LOVE YOU

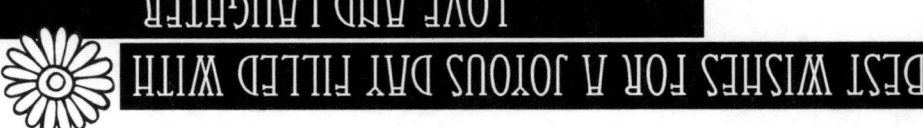

BEST WISHES FOR A JOYOUS DAY FILLED WITH LOVE AND LAUGHTER.

Freebird Publishers
www.FreebirdPublishers.com

Happy Birthday!

I hope that your special day is full of fun, happiness and everything that you enjoy.

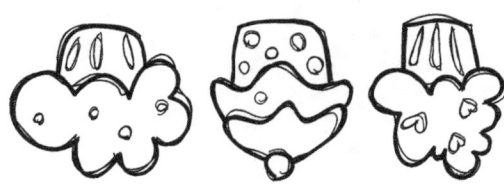

FREEBIRD PUBLISHERS
REFERENCE BOOKS

Only $26.99
includes S/H with tracking
SOFTCOVER, 6" x 9", 175+ pages

Being a Pro Se Prisoner is a mindset. Do it yourself prisoners who go and get knowledge, money and freedom. We were told that prison and DOC would rehabilitate us with programs, school, and re-entry programs. That hasn't happened, and as such the system hasn't served its purpose. With this book you will have taken the first step to empowering yourself to become financially free. Pro Se Prisoner: How to Buy Stocks & Bitcoin will allow you to learn about your financial freedom, investment options, how to buy DRIPS's, cryptocurrency and ETF's. These pages are more than a book they're the start of your journey into different investments that you probably thought weren't available to you until now. In prison you can buy stocks, bitcoins, and ETF's without having people on the outside lying to you about not having the time to help. Become a Pro Se Prisoner and put the power back into your hands.

Only $26.99
includes S/H with tracking
SOFTCOVER, 8" x 10", 240+ pages

Success in life is about becoming what you want to be. You may have heard money is the root of all evil, I don't believe that this is the case. Some people do not truly understand the concept of money. As an adult, I now realize that there is nothing wrong with wanting to be financially free, rich, or wealthy. If you also desire this then it only means that you crave a wealthier, fuller, and more abundant life than what you are currently enduring.

To become financially successful, you need to stop thinking of spending and think more on investing and acquiring assets. If not then you will continue to stay in the typical lifestyle of working for money, paying taxes, and hoping that circumstances will change (i.e., hitting the lottery or getting a substantial raise in pay). Once you begin to see money for what it is, a tool to invest, you can begin to achieve greater financial success.
Covering: Credit, Investing, Trading, Real Estate, Asset Protection and more!

Only $23.99
includes S/H with tracking
SOFTCOVER, 6" x 9", 200+ pages

Being incarcerated is hard enough on its own without dealing with the other inmates, this is where most of the stress comes from while incarcerated. HELP IS HERE! In this new book, Prisoner's Communication Guideline for Navigating in Prison has years of experience, knowledge and research on every page. Prisoners from all over the country have contributed unique points of view and successful strategies for verbally and non-verbally existing in prison during your sentence and return to society.

Whether you are truly interested in becoming an effective communicator or just improving your skills, this is the book for you. Apply the topics discussed in this book and be able to earn more privileges, make more money and get along better with fellow convicts and staff alike. Do not delay any longer, get started today. Really apply yourself and you are bound for success!

No Order Form Needed: Clearly write on paper & send with payment to:

Freebird Publishers 221 Pearl St., Ste. 541, North Dighton, MA 02764
Diane@FreebirdPublishers.com   www.Freebirdpublishers.com
We accept all forms of payment. Plus Venmo & CashApp!
Venmo: @FreebirdPublishers   CashApp: $FreebirdPublishers

THE ART of Origami

Did you know that origami came from the Japanese words "Oru" meaning "to fold" and "kami" meaning "paper"? And that is exactly what we do here - fold paper! There is quite a joy that can be achieved when you transform a plain square piece of paper into a container, animal, flower, etc. Plus, origami artwork can be a great gift for your pen pal.

Box

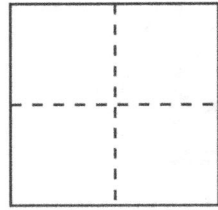

1. Start with a square piece of paper, white side up
Fold the paper in half horizontally and then verically, so the creases look like this.

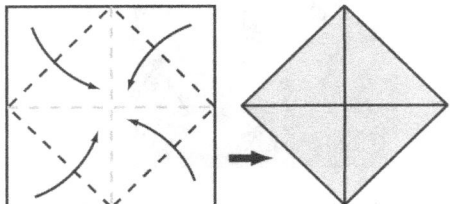

2. Fold the four corners of the paper toward the center point

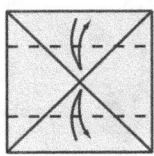

3. Fold the top and bottom of this square into the center and open out again to create these creases.

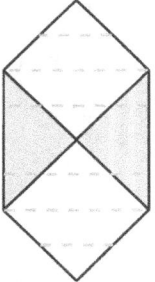

4. Open out the top and bottom triangle flaps

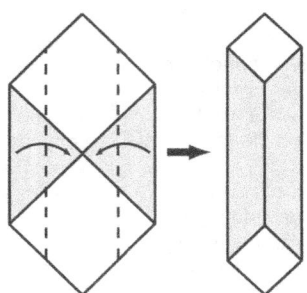

5. Fold the sides of the model into the centre, creasing well.

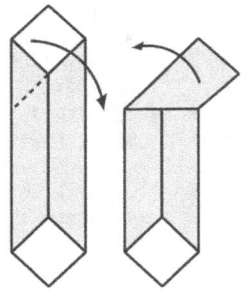

6. Fold down top corner of model and then open out again.

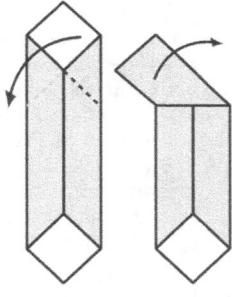

7. Fold down model in the other direction

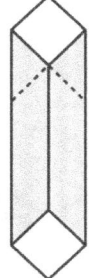

You should now have 2 new diagonal creases like this.

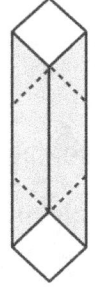

8. Repeat step 6 & 7 at the other end of the model, so you have the new creases at both ends, as shown.

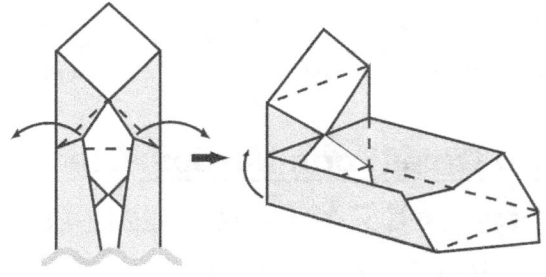

9. At one end of the model,
Open out model along the creases you just made. This will raise the top portion of the model vertically.

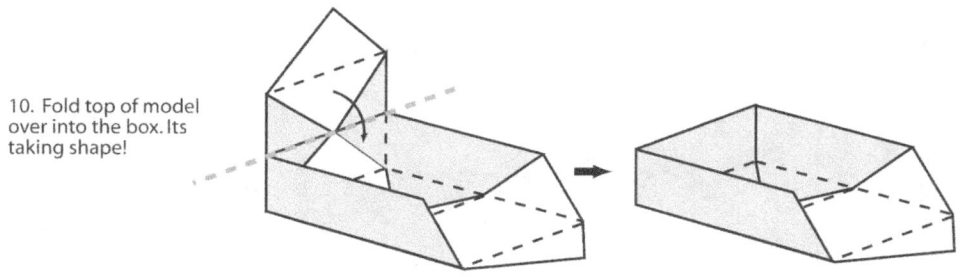

10. Fold top of model over into the box. Its taking shape!

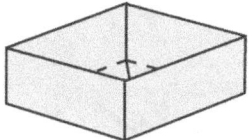

11. Repeat Step 9 and 10 at the other end of the box... and its finished!

To make a lid, just make another box, but start with a slightly bigger piece of paper.

Flower - Rose

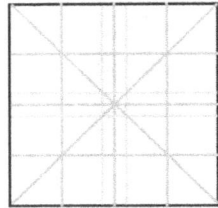

1. Make these creases.

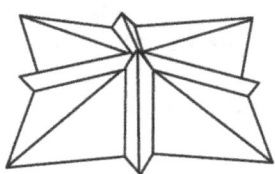

2. Form the 4 corners.

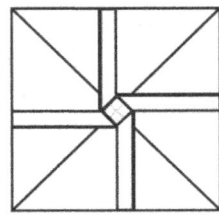

3. Flatten, while rotating counter-clockwise.

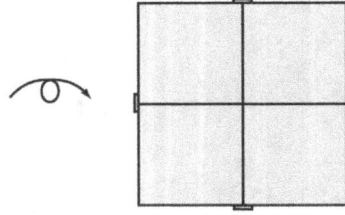

4. Turn over.

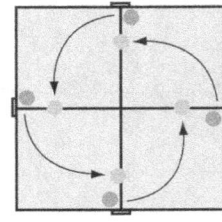
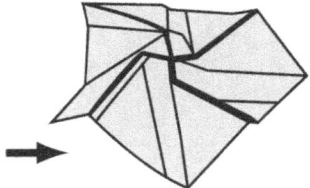

5. Form the 3D rose by taking each top right corner and folding to next quadrant, counter clockwise.

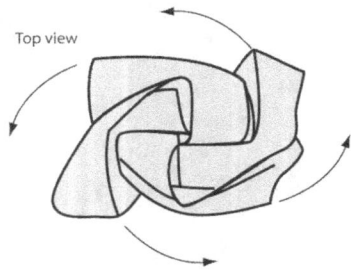

6. Form rose within the palm of your hand.

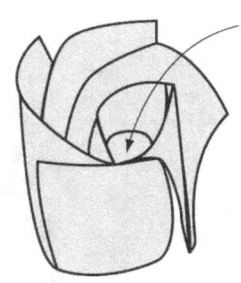

7. Turn over and smooth inside of rose, by pressing down slightly at the base.

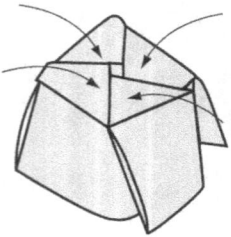

8. Fold down edges and tuck in to form the bottom of the rose.

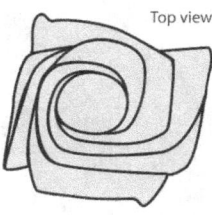

9. Turn over, open centre of flower and smooth.

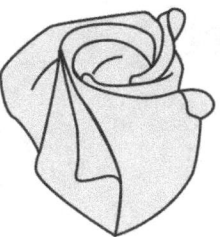

10. Roll the petals down to curve them. Finished Rose.

Flower - Lily/Iris

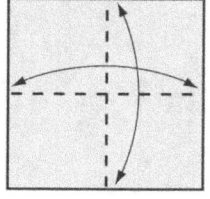 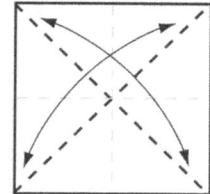 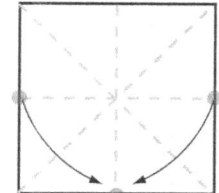

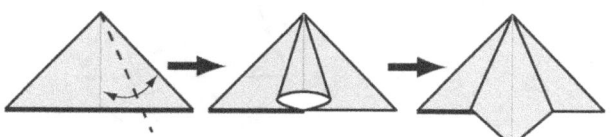  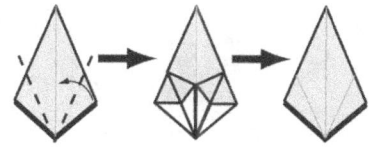

4. Fold the top triangle into the centre and unfold. Using this crease, open out the triangle and flatten.

5. You'll need to repeat step 4 on all four of the flaps of the waterbomb base. The model will now look like this.

6. On the uppermost diamond, fold the outside corners into the centre line, crease well then open.

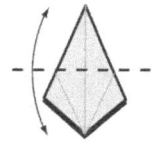  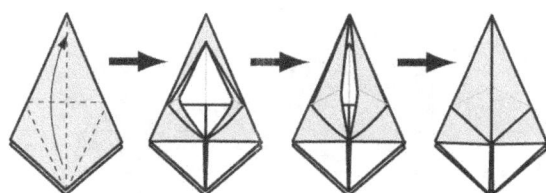

7. Fold the model in half and open.

8. Using the creases made in step 6 and 7, lift the bottom point of the model (the uppermost layer only) up to the top point, bringing in the sides of the model at the same time, as shown.

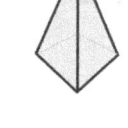 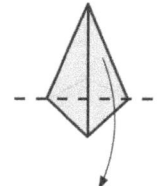 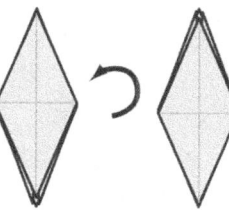 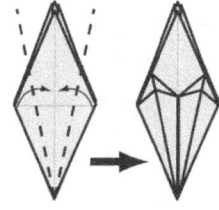

9. Repeat steps 6, 7 and 8 on each if the four sides. The model should now look like this.

10. Now fold down each of these triangles, on all four sides.

11. Rotate model upside down.

12. Fold the outer flaps toward the centre and flatten.

 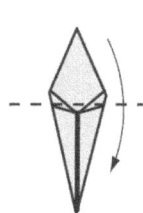 

13. Repeat step 12 on all four sides of the model. The model should now look like this.

14. Fold down all petals. Completed Lily!

Pen Pals: A Personal Guide for Prisoners

Flower - Stem/Leaf

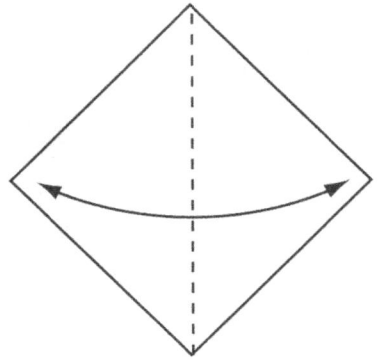

1. Start with a green square, white side up.

Fold in half, crease and open.

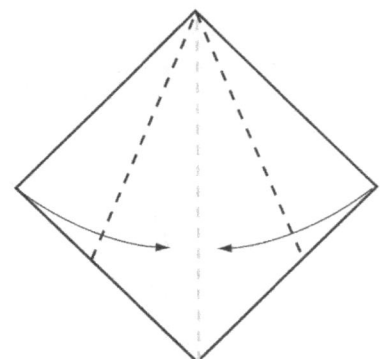

2. Fold these 2 opposite corners into the centre crease.

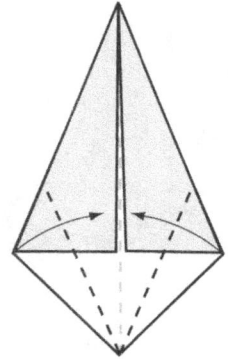

3. Fold these outer corners to the centre crease.

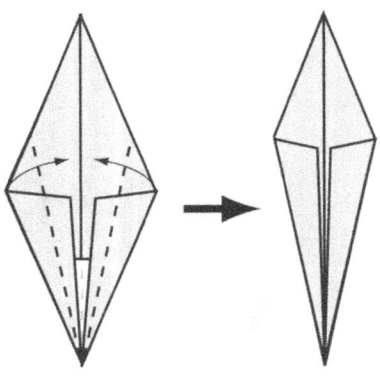

4. Again, fold outer corners to centre crease.

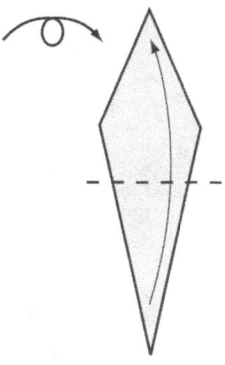

5. Turn model over and fold bottom up to the top corner.

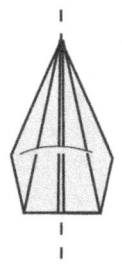

6. Now fold in half.

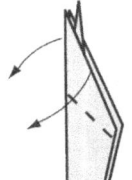

7. Crease as shown, on the front and the back.

Then use these creases to outside reverse fold the leaf.

Finished Flower Stem.
This model should stand on its own.

Can be used for any origami flower which has a hole in the base, such as the tulip. Just insert the stem into the base of the flower.

Modular Star

You will need 6 small sheets of square paper to make this star.

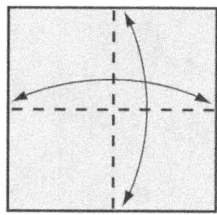

1. Start with your paper coloured side up.

Fold in half, then in half again, as shown. Crease well, then open out again.

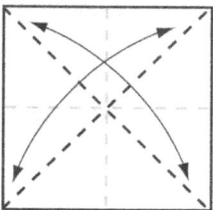

2. Turn the paper over and fold in half diagonally and in both directions. Crease well and open out once again.

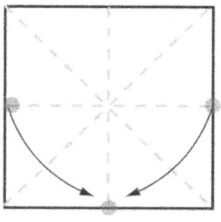
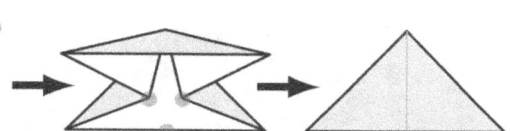

3. Holding the points shown, bring them both down to the centre point on the bottom line.

Flatten model.

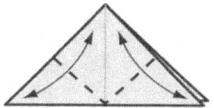

4. Fold bottom corners of top layer only to top point and unfold.
Repeat on back.
This is one module.

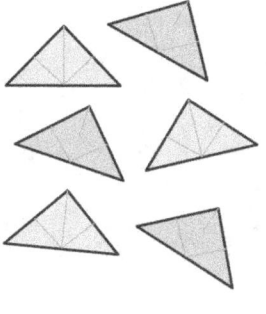

5. Make 5 more modules so you have 6 altogether.

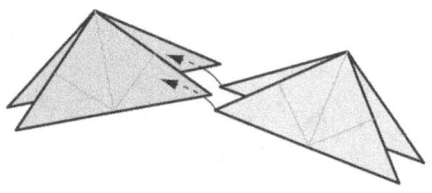

6. To join modules, slip one set of "legs'" into another set of legs, like so:

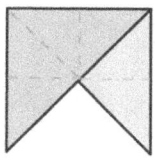

7. Push the legs in as far as they will go.

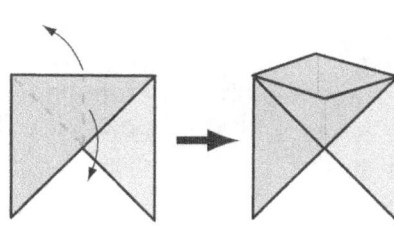

8. Pull the centre crease outwards, making it into a mountain fold.

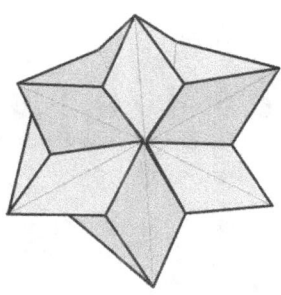

9. Continue to add modules to build the star, repeating steps 6-8 as you go.

Finished Modular Star.

Heart

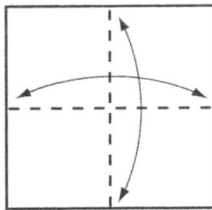 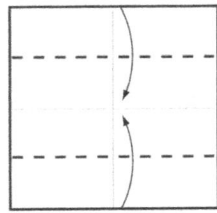 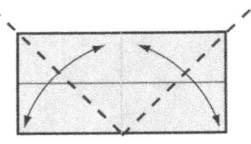

1. Start with your paper white side up.
Fold in half and unfold.
Fold in half the opposite way and unfold.

2. Fold the top and the bottom edges into the centre line

3. Fold the two bottom corners up to the top centre point and unfold

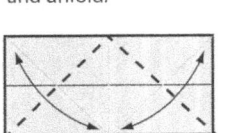 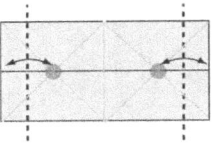 

4. Now fold the 2 top corners down to the bottom centre point and unfold.

5. Fold the outside edges in to the points shown and unfold.

6. Fold all four corners in to the creases just made.

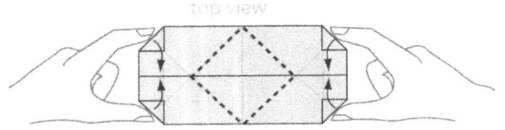 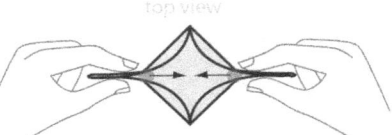 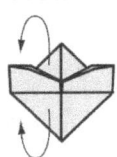

7. Now we are going to form the heart. Hold the model by the corners, as shown, and bring these corners together

8. Still holding the model together, bring the outside edges toward each other.

9. The model should now look like this.
Push the bottom diamond together underneath the model.

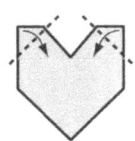  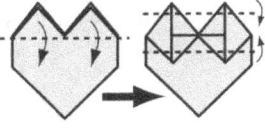 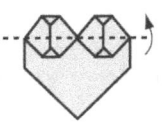

10. Lay flat on the table. Fold the two top corners down to the crease and unfold

11. Use these creases to inside reverse fold these corners.

12. Fold the uppermost flaps down. Then fold the tips inward

13. Fold the triangles back up.

Interested in more origami?

The following books are available for purchase through Freebird Publishers. Send orders to Freebird Publishers | 221 Pearl St, Ste. 541 | North Dighton, MA 02764. Price includes S/H.

 Uber Origami

$34.99

 Easy Origami

$20.99

 Beautiful Origami Flowers

$30.99

Quotes to share with your PENPAL

QUOTES *for Inspiration*

The best preparation for tomorrow is doing your best today. -Jackson Brown, Jr.

Start by doing what's necessary; then do what's possible; and suddenly you are doing the impossible. -Francis of Assisi

Perfection is not attainable, but if we chase perfection we can catch excellence. -Vince Lombardi

Try to be a rainbow in someone's cloud. -Maya Angelou

As we express our gratitutde, we must never forget that the highest appreciation is not to utter words, but to live by them. -John F. Kennedy

No act of kindness, no matter how small, is ever wasted. -Aesop

Happiness is not something you postone for the future; it is something you design for the present. -Jim Rohn

The best way out is always through. -Robert Frost

Out of difficulties grow miricles. -Jean de la Bruyere

Failure will never overtake me if my determination to succeed is strong enough. -Og Mandino

Don't watch the clock; do what it does. Keep going. -Sam Levenson

Our greatest weakness lies in giving up. The most certain way to succeed is always to try just one more time. -Thomas A. Edison

Go confidently in the direction of your dreams. Live the life you have imagined. -Henry David Thoreau

If you don't go after what you want, you'll never have it. If you don't ask, the answer is always no. If you don't step forward, you're always in the same place. -Nora Roberts

Be happy in the moment, that's enough. Each moment is all we need, not more. -Mother Teresa

Life is about making an impact, not making an income. -Kevin Kruse

Whatever the mind of a man can concieve and believe, it can achieve. -Napoleon Hill

Strive not to be a success, but rather to be of value. -Albert Einstein

Every strike brings me closer to the next home run. -Babe Ruth

Life isn't about getting and having, it's about giving and being. -Kevin Kruse

Twenty years from now you will be more disappointed by the things that you didn't do than by the ones you did do, so throw off the bowlines, sail away from safe harbor, catch the trade winds in your sails. Explore, Dream, Discover. -Mark Twain

Life is 10% what happens to me and 90% of how I react to it. -Charles Swindoll

Your time is limited, so don't waste it living someone else's life. -Steve Jobs

You can never cross the ocean until you have the courage to lose sight of the shore. -Christopher Columbus

The best revenge is massive success. -Frank Sinatra

Life shrinks or expands in proportion to one's courage. -Anais Nin

Fall seven times a day and stand up eight. -Japanese Proverb

Believe you can and you're halfway there. -Theodore Roosevelt

I didn't fail the test. I just found 100 ways to do it wrong. -Benjamin Franklin

We must believe that we are gifted for something, and that this thing, at whatever cost, must be attained. -Marie Curie

Too many of us are not living our dreams because we are living our fears. -Les Brown

It is never too late to be what you might have been. -George Eliot

QUOTES about Success

Success is not final, failure is not fatal: it is the courage to continue that counts.
-Winston Churchill

Try not to become a man of success, but rather try to become a man of value. -Albert Einstein

Success is how high you bounce when you hit bottom. -George S. Patton

Don't aim for success if you want it; just do what you love and believe in, and it will come naturally. -David Frost

Success consists of going from failure to failure without loss of enthusiasm. -Winston Churchill

Success is to be measured not so much by the position that one has reached in life as by the obstacles which he has overcome. -Booker T. Washington

Always bear in mind that your own resolution to succeed is more important than any other.
-Abraham Lincoln

Think twice before you speak, because your words and influence will plant the seed of either success or failure in the mind of another.
-Napoleon Hill

If you set your goals ridiculously high and it's a failure, you will fail above everyone else's success. -James Cameron

All our dreams can come true if we have the courage to pursue them. -Walt Disney

Opportunities don't happen. You create them.
-Chris Grosser

A successful man is one who can lay a firm foundation with the bricks others have thrown him. -David Brinkley

No one can make you feel inferior without your consent. -Eleanor Roosevelt

Don't be afraid to give up the good to go for the great. -John D. Rockerfeller

The only place where success comes before work is in the dictionary. -Vidal Sassoon

I don't know the key to success, but the key to failure is trying to please everyone. -Bill Cosby

All progress takes place outside the comfort zone. -Michael John Bobak

What seems to us as bitter trials are often blessings in disguise. -Oscar Wilde

Motivation is what gets you started. Habit is what keeps you going. -Jim Ryun

Our greatest fear should not be of failure...but of succeeding at things in life that don't really matter. -Francis Chan

Be patient with yourself. Self-growth is tender; its holy ground. There's no greater investment.
-Stephen Covey

Logic will get you from A to B. Imagination will take you everywhere. -Albert Einstein

Success is just a war of attrition. Sure, there's an element of talent you should probably possess. But if you just stick around long enough, eventually something is going to happen. -Dax Shepard

My tombstone? I'm thinking something along the lines of, 'Geez, he was just here a minute ago."
-George Carlin

The greatest artists like Dylan, Picasso and Newton risked failure. And if we want to be great, we've got to risk it too. -Steve Jobs

It [what you choose to do] has got to be something that you're passionate about because otherwise you won't have the perserverance to see it through. -Steve Jobs

Doing the best at this moment puts you in the best place for the next moment. -Oprah Winfrey

I do not know the word 'quit'. Either I never did, or I have abolished it. -Susan Butcher

Life is either a daring adventure or nothing.
-Helen Keller

So be sure when you step, step with care and great tact. And remember that life's a great balancing act. And you will succeed? Yes! You will, indeed! (98 and 3/4 percent guaranteed) Kid, you'll move mountains. -Dr. Seuss

Your friendship is a SPECIAL GIFT generously given, happily accepted & DEEPLY appreciated

Friends are ANGELS that lift us to our feet when our wings have TROUBLE REMEMBERING to Fly

QUOTES about Friendship

A real friend is one who walks in when the rest of the world walks out. -Walter Winchell

Friendship is always a sweet responsibility, never an opportunity. -Khalil Gilbran

A single rose can be my garden...a single friend, my world. -Leo Buscaglia

Friendship is unnecessary, like philosophy, like art...It has no survival value; rather it is one of those things that give value to survival. -C.S. Lewis

Two persons cannot long be friends if they cannot forgive each other's little failings. -Jean de la Bruyere

Let us be grateful to people who make us happy, they are the charming gardeners who make our souls blossom. - Marcel Proust

A true friend is someone who sees the pain in your eyes while everyone else believes the smile on your face. -unknown

Best friends are connected heart to heart distance will never break them apart. -unknown

Walking with a friend in the dark is better than walking alone in the light. -Helen Keller

A friend is one that knows you as you are, understands where you have been, accepts what you have become, and still, gently allows you to grow. -William Shakespeare

Don't walk behind me; I may not lead. Don't walk in front of me; I may not follow. Just walk beside me and be my friend. -Albert Camus

The only way to have friends is to be one. -Ralph Waldo Emerson

A friend is someone who gives you total freedom to be yourself. -Jim Morrison

True friendship comes when the silence between two people is comfortable. -David Tyson Gentry

Be slow to fall into friendship; but when thou art in, continue firm and constant. -Socrates

Sweet is the memory of distant friends! Like the mellow rays of the departing sun, it falls tenderly, yet sadly, on the heart. -Washington Irving

Growing apart doesn't change the fact that for a long time we grew side by side; our roots will always be tangled. I'm glad for that. -Ally Condie

Friends are the family you choose. -Jess C. Scott

We cannot tell the precise moment when friendship is formed. As in filling a vessel drop by drop, there is at last a drop which makes it run over; so in a series of kindnesses there is at last one which makes the heart run over. -Ray Bradbury

Tis the privilege of friendship to talk nonsense, and have her nonsense respected. -Charles Lamb

True friends never apart, maybe in distance, but never in heart. -Helen Keller

Sometimes, the people who are thousands of miles away from you, can make you feel better than the people right beside you. -unknown

A strong friendship doesn't need daily conversations, doesn't always need togetherness, as long as the relationship lives in the heart, true friends will never part... -unknown

A best friend is like a four leaf clover, hard to find and lucky to have. -Sarah Jessica Parker (Sex and the City Tv Series)

Friends are like stars, they come and go, but the ones that stay are the ones that glow. -Roxy Quicksilver

Each friend represents a world in us, a world possibly not born until they arrive, and it is only by this meeting that a new world is born. -Anais Nin

The greatest good you can do for another is not just share your riches, but to reveal to him, his own. -Benjamin Disraeli

If you judge people, you have no time to love them. -Mother Teresa

Misfortune shows those who are not really friends. -Aristotle

Pen Pals: A Personal Guide for Prisoners

LOVE IS NOT BLIND it simply ENABLES ONE to SEE THINGS OTHERS FAIL to see.

IN DREAMS and IN LOVE there are no IMPOSSIBILITIES

the GREATEST Thing YOU'LL LEARN is to Love AND BE LOVED IN RETURN

Love doesn't make the WORLD Go ROUND Love is what makes THE RIDE Worth Living

QUOTES about Love

Love isn't something you find. Love is something that finds you. -Loretta Young

Love is when another person's happiness is more important than your own. -H. Jackson Brown, Jr.

Love is friendship that has caught fire. It is quiet understanding, mutual confidence, sharing and forgiving. It is loyalty through good and bad times. it settles for less than perfection and makes allowances for human weaknesses.

You can't blame gravity for falling in love. -Albert Einstein

Love is life. And if you miss love, you miss life. -Leo Buscaglia

Being deeply loved by someone gives you strength, while loving someone deeply gives you courage.

Love is when he gives you a piece of your soul, that you never knew was missing. -Torquato Tasso

You know when you're in love when you can't fall asleep because reality is finally better than your dreams. -Dr. Seuss

Once you truly believe you're worthy of love, you will never settle for anyone's second best treatment. -Charles J. Orlando

When you trip over love, it is easy to get up. But when you fall in love, it is impossible to stand again. -Albert Einstein

And remember, as it was written, to love another person is to see the face of God. -Les Miserables

When you realize you want to spend the rest of your life with somebody, you want the rest of your life to start as soon as possible. -When Harry Met Sally

We are most alive when we're in love. -John Updike

The greater your capacity to love, the greater your capicity to feel the pain. -Jennifer Aniston

I have decided to stick to love; hate is too great a burden to bear. -Martin Luther King, Jr.

Better to have lost and loved than never to have loved at all. -Hemingway

I fell in love the way you fall asleep: slowly, and then all at once. -John Green

I would rather have eyes that cannot see; ears that cannot hear; lips that cannot speak, than a heart that cannot love.

For you see, each day I love you more. Today more than yesterday and less than tomorrow. -Rosemonde Gerard

I've fallen in love many times...always with you. -unkown

Love me when I least deserve it, because that's when I really need it. -Swedish Proverb

People will forget what you said. People will forget what you did. But people will never forget how you made them feel. -Maya Angelou

The heart has its reasons of which reason knows nothing. -Blaise Pascal

You come to love not by finding the perfect person, but by learning to see an imperfect person perfectly. -Sam Keen

Don't look for big things, just do small things with great love. -Mother Teresa

To love someone deeply gives you strength. Being loved by someone deeply gives you courage. -Lao Tzu

The best love is the kind that awakens the soul, that makes us reach for more, that plants the fire in our hearts and brings peace to our minds. That's what I hope to give you forever. -Nicholas Sparks, The Notebook

Our love is like the wind -- you can't see it, but you can feel it.

Love is like a virus. It can happen to anybody at any time. -Maya Angelou

Don't settle for a relationship that won't let you be yourself. -Oprah Winfrey

Pen Pals: A Personal Guide for Prisoners

OPPORTUNITIES HAPPEN — if **YOU** DON'T create them

The HARDER THE CONFLICT, THE MORE GLORIOUS THE TRIUMPH

YOU WILL KNOW YOUR **NEVER** Limits until you push YOURSELF TO THEM

SPEED LIMIT 35

THE BEST WAY TO PREDICT **THE FUTURE** IS TO CREATE IT!

PENPAL *Stationary*

PENPAL

Using stationary ensures your letter is delivered in style! Tear out the following pages (or make copies) for your personal pen pal use. Each page has a back which coordinates with the front lined page. Feel free to add your own color to these (some have definitely been designed specifically for that intent).

For help on how to cleanly remove the pull out pages of this book refer to page 74.

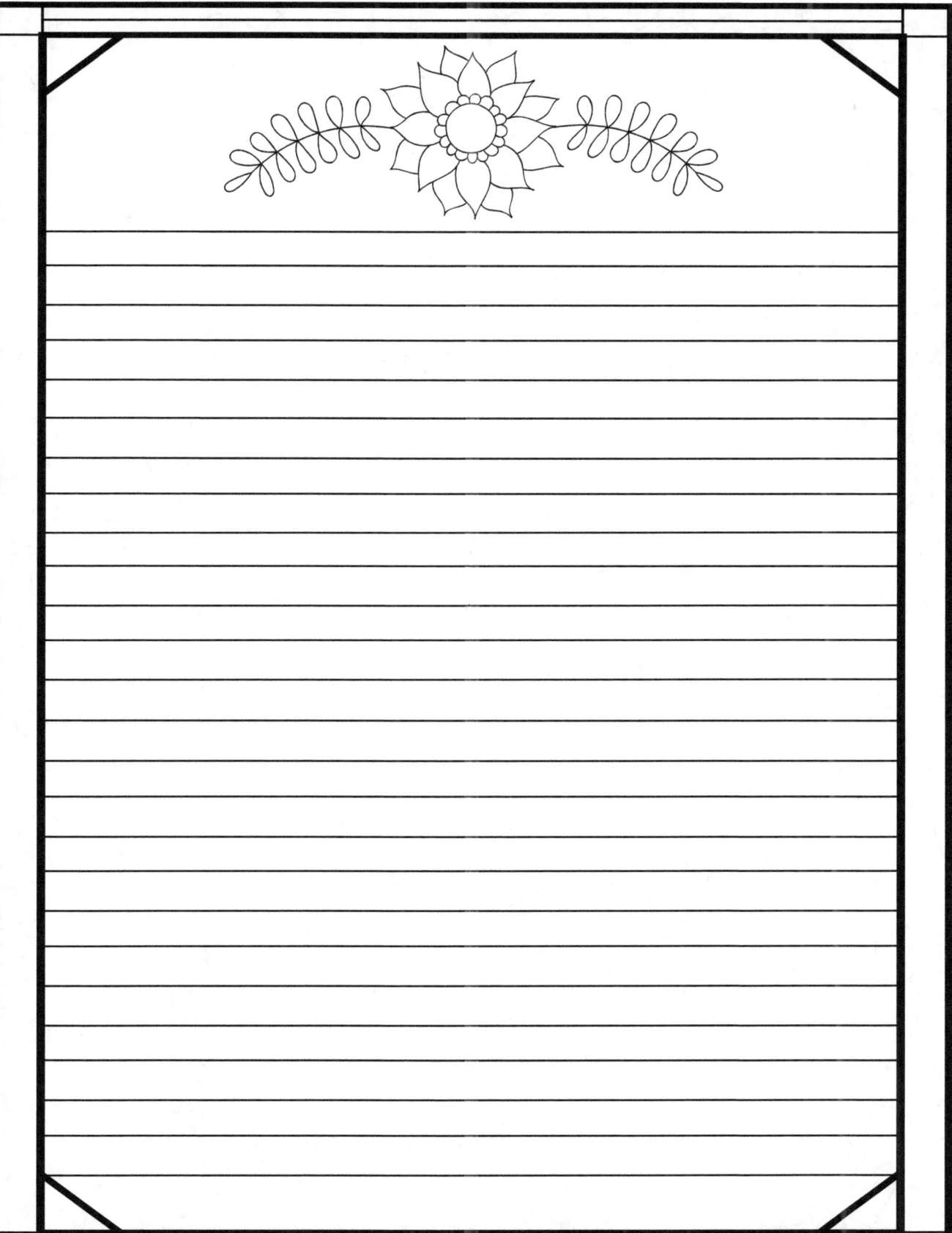

The best and most beautiful things in the world cannot be seen or even touched - they must be felt with the heart.

Helen Keller

Just when the caterpiller thought the world was over, it became a butterfly.

The best relationships usually begin unexpectedly.

I'M Lucky ·TO· HAVE YOU

But friendship is
the breathing rose,
with sweets in every fold.

PENPAL
Happiness

PENPAL *Happiness*

Finding that special pen pal will make all your efforts worth while. Here are some pen pal stories with happy endings. Hopefully this will inspire you to continue in your pen pal journey until you find yours.

> " I am a 36 year old woman with 3 kids from my previous marrage. My husband and I divorced 8 years ago and I was lonely until I met Nicholas from Michigan. I found him on a pen pal site some time ago. We wrote to each other for 3 years before finally meeting. Upon his release Nicholas came to California and he stayed here for 4 weeks in the summer. It was like I'd known him for years, we would sit up all night and talk about anything, our conversations just went on and on. Well finally Nicholas moved here to California and we were dating for a further 4 years before we got married. Now we are living in Colorado with my 3 kids and we have 2 kids of our own. Thanks to the pen pal website, I met my perfect partner. "
>
> *Michelle*

> " One day when I was bored I started searching the internet looking for someone to connect with. I'd tried chat rooms, online games and it just seemed to provide me with shallow conversations with people who weren't looking for any sort of meaningful connections. Somehow I stumbled across an article about becoming a pen pal with a prisoner. I have to say at first I was sceptical. I began looking through profile after profile and hours flew by. I decided to write a few different people just to see what it was all about. Thats where I met Reynoldo. He was the most down to earth, kind hearted man. We exchanged letters for a few years before I officially met him. We still continue our relationship through written letter, phone calls and the occassional visits. He's been there for me since day one with nothing but love and respect. I don't know what I'd do if I didn't have him. "
>
> *Cynthia*

> " Every guy whose down and lonely knows about the pen pal sites. We've all tried them, but I have one great success story. I've met many different women by being listed on pen pal websites. There's been the ones that write one letter and they're gone, and then there are the everlasting ones that you consider changing your life for. Nyquan was my sun in the darkest of times. She's provided me with an escape from this terrible existence and given me a reason to get out of bed every morning. Next month I will be meeting my true love for the first time. "
>
> *Jamal*

> " I met Robert almost two years ago thanks to a prison pen pal website. I was skeptical in finding a companion but gave it a try. Since then Robert has changed my life, taught me to love myself and others, as well as creating an unbreakable bond with such an amazing person. Meeting him was a choice but falling in love was fate. We are working together to overturn his case and we hope prayers are answered because I cannot imagine spending the rest of my life with him behind bars. He has become my best friend, my counselor, my reason to smile on most days. I've learned that you can never judge a person for what they have done, you must get to know the real person trapped behind closed doors. Thank you so much for opening my eyes to a world I may never have seen! "
>
> *Shelby*

> " I first wrote Richard after watching a program on television about prisoners and their lives behind bars. I certainly wasn't looking for love - having just come out of a long term relationship which ended on hostile terms - I wasn't even open to the idea, but I was lonely and looking for someone to talk to. I assumed that like myself prisoners must be lonely as well so I thought it only best I give it a shot.
>
> Our first letters were a bit formal. I told him I'd gotten out of a harsh relationship. He discussed his living conditions and the terrors of living inside one of America's toughest facilities. We exchanged photos early on. I was struck by his handsomeness. He wasn't at all what I'd expect of a prisoner. He comes from a fairly wealthy family who is quite lovely.
>
> Letters and letters past and I found myself thinking about him. Counting the hours and figuring out what time it would be in America and what he'd be doing at that time. We started reading books together, we would exchange poetry. We began to find more in more in common in each other and I started feeling the desire to meet him. I suggested I plan a holiday to America. My first glimpse of him was of him hugging his mother. We had gone to the prison together and as he was walking over she said "Honey, here he comes," I was so terrified I hid my head. When I looked up he was grinning at me. He picked me up and swung me around and said "Gee, you're so tiny."
>
> I was struck by how tall he was, and how much more handsome he was in person than in his photos. I have to stop thinking about it because all it does is build more and more desire - which we do not speak of since all we can do on a visit is kiss, but it's certainly there. That burning desire. 2 years, 3 days, and five hours (thereabout) cannot come quickly enough. "
>
> *Angela*

PENPAL *Happiness*

> So my friend, Cindy, has been corresponding with a prisoner in California. She and another friend decided about a year ago to be "pen pals" with different prisoners. This whole idea sketched me out from the beginning because they were using their real return addresses on the envelopes. I tried at that point convincing the friend to at least get a PO box or something so that the prisoners wouldn't know where she lived. Her response was "well he lives in California" (we are in VA). Anyways I had kind of forgotten about all of this until about a month ago. Cindy started talking about "Michael" After a few mentions of this name, I was curious---who is Michael? She said "oh that guy I talk to in prison". At this point she was talking about speaking with him on the phone. She has to pay for the calls. I will add now, Michael is in prison for a gang related murder. I don't know when he was convicted, nor how long his sentence was. He is roughly our age---31 or so. So today I was at Cindy's house and there is a small painting of her and Michael. I was like oh my God Cindy, what is that!!! It was her bday present from Michael. He paid another prisoner to paint it. She was so proud and giddy about it. I stopped her right there and said "what in the world is going on here" Her responser---I" am in love with him". My jaw dropped. Cindy is a great person with a great head on her shoulders. She and I work together, at IBM, and she just got promoted and is on track to be promoted again in a year. She grew up in tough times (raised by a single mom, welfare etc..) but has strived all of her adult life to become a well rounded person and citizen. She informs me throughout the convo that he is coming up for parole in Feb. and wants to come out here. I think for a visit. Nope, she is letting him MOVE IN WITH HER!!!! I was shocked to say the least. I didn't know what to say or how to respond. She told me that it is so different to fall in love with someone through print then in person. That you learn so much more and on a different level then you do when you are with someone. Upon Michael's release he moved in with Cindy as planned. I met him for the first time yesterday. He's sweet, humble and treats her like a queen. As hard of an idea as I found it to be, I'm happy my friend found love - even if it was in the strangest of situations.
>
> *Abby*

> One night I was surfing the internet and an ad popped up about pen pals in the United States. I browsed a few different sites before landing on penacon.com where I came across a sweet looking man named Rick. Rick was tall, handsome and everything he wrote just made me want to know him so badly. Looking at his sweet, innocent eyes I couldn't imagine how or why he would even be incarcerated. He had an extended amount of time for a non-violent (on his part) offense. It just did not make sense to me. Still does not - to this day. I wrote Rick and our letters brought us so close together, even though I'd never met him physically I began to have this intense, unexplainable connection with him. In each letter we became closer. And after hearing his amazing voice on the phone that was it - I knew then I'd love this man forever. Before long I found myself saving every bit of money I could so that I could fly over and meet him. He was every bit as wonderful as the man I fell in love with through letters. A couple of visits and several months later I received a letter in the mail with a picture of Rick down on one knee. YES. Of course I said yes. Not long after I was flying back to marry the man of my dreams. That's us on the page to the right. We're happily married and soon I will be moving close to my Ricky so I can see him every single day possible.
>
> *Jackie*

SPECIALIZING IN PRISONER PUBLICATIONS

For a 88 page FULL COLOR CATALOG filled with details of every book, gifts and services, Send $5, add $5 more for shipping/with tracking to Freebird Publishers

E-BOOKS

Prices Ranging from $2.99-$5.99
Interested in Freebird Publishers eBooks on your tablet?
Have your tablet service provider contact diane@freebirdpublishers.com

- § 2254 Pro Se Guide to Winning Federal Relief
- Ask. Believe. Receive.
- Celebrity Female Star Power
- Cell Chef Cookbook I & II
- Cellpreneur
- Chapter 7 Bankruptcy
- Convicted Creations Cookbook
- DIY For Prisoners
- Federal Rules of Criminal Procedures
- Federal Rules of Evidence
- Fine Dining Prison Cookbook 1 & 2
- Get Money – Vol.1-3
- Gift Look Book
- How to Write a Good Letter
- Ineffective Assistance of Counsel

- Inmate Shopper Annual
- Inmate Shopper Annual Censored
- Introduction to Financial Success
- Kitty Kat
- Life with a Record
- Locked Down Cookin'
- Locked Up Love Letters
- Parent to Parent
- Pen Pal Success – The Ultimate Guide to Getting & Keeping Pen Pals
- Pen Pals: A Personal Guide for Prisoners
- Pillow Talk
- Post-Conviction Relief Series (7 books)
- Prison Health Handbook
- Prison Legal Guide

- Prisoner's Communication Guide
- Pro Se Guide to Legal Research & Writing
- Pro Se Prisoner: How to Buy Stocks & Bitcoin
- S.T.O.P Start Thinking Outside Prison
- Soft Shots
- The Best 500 Non-Profit Organizations for Prisoners & Their Families
- The Habeas Corpus Manual
- The Pro Se Section 1983 Manual
- Weight Loss Unlocked
- Write & Get Paid

ALL BOOKS AVAILABLE IN PAPERBACK
ASK YOUR SERVICE PROVIDER TO CONTACT US TODAY!

FREEBIRD PUBLISHERS
221 PEARL ST., STE 541, NORTH DIGHTON, MA 02764
TEXT/PHONE 774-406-8682

NEW BOOKS PUBLISHED MONTHLY!

PENPAL
My Notes & Addresses

My Pen Pal Addresses

Name:

Address: _____
_____
_____

Phone: _____
Birthday: _____
Notes: _____
_____
_____
_____
_____
_____

Name:

Address: _____
_____
_____

Phone: _____
Birthday: _____
Notes: _____
_____
_____
_____
_____
_____

Name:

Address: _____
_____
_____

Phone: _____
Birthday: _____
Notes: _____
_____
_____
_____
_____
_____

Name:

Address: _____
_____
_____

Phone: _____
Birthday: _____
Notes: _____
_____
_____
_____
_____
_____

My Pen Pal Addresses

Name:

Address: _____

_____

_____

Phone: _____

Birthday: _____

Notes: _____

_____

_____

_____

_____

_____

Name:

Address: _____

_____

_____

Phone: _____

Birthday: _____

Notes: _____

_____

_____

_____

_____

_____

Name:

Address: _____

_____

_____

Phone: _____

Birthday: _____

Notes: _____

_____

_____

_____

_____

_____

Name:

Address: _____

_____

_____

Phone: _____

Birthday: _____

Notes: _____

_____

_____

_____

_____

_____

My Pen Pal Addresses

Name:

Address: _____
_____
_____

Phone: _____
Birthday: _____
Notes: _____
_____
_____
_____
_____
_____

Name:

Address: _____
_____
_____

Phone: _____
Birthday: _____
Notes: _____
_____
_____
_____
_____
_____

Name:

Address: _____
_____
_____

Phone: _____
Birthday: _____
Notes: _____
_____
_____
_____
_____
_____

Name:

Address: _____
_____
_____

Phone: _____
Birthday: _____
Notes: _____
_____
_____
_____
_____
_____

My Pen Pal Addresses

Name:

Address: _____
_____
_____

Phone: _____

Birthday: _____

Notes: _____
_____
_____
_____
_____
_____

Name:

Address: _____
_____
_____

Phone: _____

Birthday: _____

Notes: _____
_____
_____
_____
_____
_____

Name:

Address: _____
_____
_____

Phone: _____

Birthday: _____

Notes: _____
_____
_____
_____
_____
_____

Name:

Address: _____
_____
_____

Phone: _____

Birthday: _____

Notes: _____
_____
_____
_____
_____
_____

My Pen Pal Addresses

Name:

Address: _____
_____
_____

Phone: _____
Birthday: _____
Notes: _____
_____
_____
_____
_____
_____
_____

Name:

Address: _____
_____
_____

Phone: _____
Birthday: _____
Notes: _____
_____
_____
_____
_____
_____
_____

Name:

Address: _____
_____
_____

Phone: _____
Birthday: _____
Notes: _____
_____
_____
_____
_____
_____
_____

Name:

Address: _____
_____
_____

Phone: _____
Birthday: _____
Notes: _____
_____
_____
_____
_____
_____
_____

My Pen Pal Addresses

Name:

Address: _____
_____

Phone: _____

Birthday: _____

Notes: _____
_____
_____
_____
_____
_____

Name:

Address: _____
_____

Phone: _____

Birthday: _____

Notes: _____
_____
_____
_____
_____
_____

Name:

Address: _____
_____

Phone: _____

Birthday: _____

Notes: _____
_____
_____
_____
_____
_____

Name:

Address: _____
_____

Phone: _____

Birthday: _____

Notes: _____
_____
_____
_____
_____
_____

My Pen Pal Addresses

Name:

Address: _____
_____
_____

Phone: _____
Birthday: _____
Notes: _____
_____
_____
_____
_____
_____

Name:

Address: _____
_____
_____

Phone: _____
Birthday: _____
Notes: _____
_____
_____
_____
_____
_____

Name:

Address: _____
_____
_____

Phone: _____
Birthday: _____
Notes: _____
_____
_____
_____
_____
_____

Name:

Address: _____
_____
_____

Phone: _____
Birthday: _____
Notes: _____
_____
_____
_____
_____
_____

Soft Shots Vol. I
NON-NUDE PHOTOS
WWW.FREEBIRDPUBLISHERS.COM

Freebird Publishers
Non-Nude Photo Book

- Over 100 photos
- 5.25 x 8 inch
- 150 Pages
- Full Color
- Non Nude
- Prison Friendly

NO ORDER FORM NEEDED

On paper clearly write your full contact information and what you are ordering.

Only $33.99 includes s/h w/tracking

Send $33.99 to: Freebird Publishers
Mail to: 221 Pearl St., Ste 541
North Dighton, MA 02764

PILLOW TALK NON-NUDE PHOTO BOOK

$33.99 INCLUDES S/H

These attractive and sexy girls will keep you company at any time of day. They will pick you up in the mornings and put some pep in your step in the afternoons. For when the long evenings come around these beauties are at their best with pillow talk.

Come see our beautiful ladies dressed in the tiniest of outfits and posing in many different alluring positions.

Full color gloss non-nude photos. A different photo on every page. Over $100+ worth of sexy photos in one book, for one low price. Non-nude prison friendly.

- Over 100 Photos
- 5.25 x 8 inches
- 150 Pages
- Full Color
- Non Nude
- Prison Friendly

NO ORDER FORM NEEDED ON PAPER CLEARLY WRITE YOUR FULL CONTACT INFORMATION AND WHAT YOU ARE ORDERING.

SEND $33.99 TO:
FREEBIRD PUBLISHERS
221 Pearl St., Ste. 541
North Dighton, MA 02764
Info@FreebirdPublishers.com
www.FreebirdPublishers.com

We accept all forms of payments.
All credit cards, MoneyGraqm and
Paypal.me/FreebirdPublishers

FREEBIRD PUBLISHERS
PEN PAL BOOKS

Only $31.99
Includes S/H with Tracking
SOFTCOVER, 8" x 10", 260 pages

Only $31.99
Includes S/H with Tracking
SOFTCOVER, 8" x 10", 200 pages

You've heard it said "The game is to be sold not told." Well, now a new book is doing all the telling about the game.
In 20 information-dense chapters you'll DISCOVER the following secrets:

- How to find FREE pen pals that are willing to write to prisoners.
- Make money legally in the pen pal game without running any bogus prison scams.
- Effectively use online pen pal websites.
- What to do once you get your pen pal so you can them on your team for years!
- How to write letters to pen pals that get you responses!
- Learn the website the author used to get 20+ hits in the first week his profile was up.
- How to rekindle a lost pen pal correspondence and keep pen pals coming back for more.
- The act of gift giving so you don't look like a trick-off artist;

What's more, this book is jam-packed with the full contact information of people and companies that can help you succeed today!

AND THERE'S MUCH, MUCH MORE!

Resources, Tips, Creative Inspiration and much more!
A guide designed to help prisoners keep their pen pals interested and coming back for more. With resources, tips, and creative inspiration you're sure to hang on to your pen pals.

- Pen Pal Resources for Prisoners
- Pen Pal Resources for Anyone
- Pen Pal Specialized Resources
- Pen Pal Profiles & Writing Tips
- Creating Your Profile
- Writing Your First Letter
- Pen Pal Etiquette
- 100 Things to Tell Your Pen Pal
- 100 Getting to Know You Questions
- How to Keep It Interesting
- How to Improve Your Handwriting
- How to Start & Close Your Letter
- How to Write a Love Letter
- Pen Pal Mail Art & Ideas
- Envelope Art & Ideas
- Fonts / Lettering
- Hand Lettering
- Doodles & Embellishments
- Make Your Own Greeting Cards
- The Art of Origami
- Quotes to Share with Your Pen Pal
- Pen Pal Stationary
- My Pen Pal Notes & Address Book Section

No Order Form Needed: Clearly write on paper & send with payment to:

Freebird Publishers 221 Pearl St., Ste 541, North Dighton, MA 02764
Diane@FreebirdPublishers.com   www.Freebirdpublishers.com
We accept all forms of payment. Plus Venmo & CashApp!
Venmo: @FreebirdPublishers   CashApp: $FreebirdPublishers

2 MUST HAVE BOOKS FOR PRISONERS

$29.99
$20.99 plus $9 Shipping/Handling with Tracking

$26.99
$17.99 plus $9 Shipping/Handling with Tracking

NO ORDER FORM NEEDED
Clearly write on paper and send with payment.
Freebird Publishers, 221 North Dighton, MA 02764

INMATE SHOPPER
- Non-Nude Girls
- Pen Pal Resources
- Social Media
- Magazine Sellers
- Text/Phone
- Catalogs to Order
- Sexy Photo Sellers
- Typists
- Personal Assistants
- Gift Shops
- Publishing Services
- LGBTQ Resources

GET BOTH FOR JUST **$47.99** INCLUDES PRIORITY S/H WITH TRACKING

ORDER THE COMBO & SAVE!! $$

THE BEST 500+
- Legal: Innocence, Research, Advocates, Copies
- Newsletters
- Educational
- Health & Healthcare
- Reentry & Jobs
- Family & Children
- Veterans
- Sentencing Issues
- LGBTQ Resources
- Newsletter & Books
- & Much Much More!

EVERY ISSUE CONTAINS

INCLUDES MANY RESOURCES

ALSO AVAILABLE FOR PURCHASE AT FREEBIRDPUBLISHERS.COM